BASIC DOCUMENTS IN MEDIEVAL HISTORY

NORTON DOWNS

Associate Professor of History
Trinity College
Hartford, Connecticut

AN ANVIL ORIGINAL

under the general editorship of

LOUIS L. SNYDER

D. VAN NOSTRAND COMPANY, INC.

PRINCETON, NEW JERSEY

TORONTO   LONDON

NEW YORK

To

My Dear Wife and Children

D. VAN NOSTRAND COMPANY, INC.
120 Alexander St., Princeton, New Jersey (*Principal office*); 24 West 40 St., New York, N.Y.
D. VAN NOSTRAND COMPANY (Canada), LTD.
25 Hollinger Rd., Toronto 16, Canada
D. VAN NOSTRAND COMPANY, LTD.
358, Kensington High Street, London, W.14, England

Library of Congress Catalog Card No. 59-9758

PREFACE

THIS collection of basic documents in medieval history has been compiled for students who, for one reason or another, are unable to make use of them in the language in which they were written. They help reveal the vast energy and activity of this period in law, constitutional development, the church, education, and social and economic change. Nothing can take the place of original documents for they are the actual records of people contemporary to the event.

I would like to express my thanks to the general editor of the Anvil Series, Professor Snyder, and the publisher, particularly Mr. E. M. Crane, Jr., for their many kindnesses. My thanks go also to the Librarian and staff of the Trinity College and Watkinson Libraries.

Hartford, Conn.
February, 1959   NORTON DOWNS

ACKNOWLEDGMENTS

THE editor has been placed under great obligation to the following publishers for permission to reprint documents that appeared in books published by them. The editor expresses his thanks to those who are listed below, and also to the scholars of the past, especially Bishop William Stubbs, Dana C. Munro, and Ernest F. Henderson, for without their labors this volume would not have been possible.

Random House, Inc., for the passages from Tacitus.

Princeton University Press for selections from Henry Goddard Leach, *A Pageant of Old Scandinavia;* Clyde Pharr, trans., *The Theodosian Code*.

Oxford University Press for selections from Henry Bettenson, *Documents of the Christian Church*.

Cambridge University Press for a selection from F. L. Attenborough, *The Laws of the Earliest English Kings*.

University of Pennsylvania Press for selections from the *Translations and Reprints from the Original Sources of European History*.

The Mediaeval Academy of America for the passage from S. H. Cross and O. P. Sherbowitz-Wetzor, *The Russian Primary Chronicle*.

Thomas Nelson & Sons, Ltd., for the letter of Innocent III from C. R. Cheney and W. H. Semple, *Selected Letters of Pope Innocent III*.

Columbia University Press for the document from W. Lunt, *Papal Revenues in the Middle Ages,* Volume II.

Eyre & Spottiswoode, for the selections from "Glanville."

Charles Scribner's Sons for documents from *A Source Book of Mediaeval History,* by Oliver J. Thatcher and Edgar H. McNeal, copyright 1905 by Charles Scribner's Sons, 1933 by Oliver J. Thatcher.

Columbia University Press for the selections from R. S. Lopez and I. W. Raymond, *Medieval Trade in the Mediterranean World* (Records of Civilization, LII, New York, 1955).

Ginn & Company for the document on German towns from James Harvey Robinson, *Readings in European History,* copyright 1904.

4

TABLE OF CONTENTS

5

THE GERMANS, FIRST CENTURY A. D.[1]

The fullest account of the customs and life of the Germans before they invaded the Roman Empire is found in the score of pages entitled Germany and Its Tribes *by Tacitus. He was a Roman aristocrat, born in the middle of the first century, who died some time after 116. His other historical writings include the long* Annals *and* History. *The pamphlet from which extracts are given below was written in 98. While he may not be correct in every point, Tacitus does present an image of the people many of whom were to enter the Roman Empire, at first in peace, and finally in the fourth century as invaders. From Britain to Italy they brought customs and traditions that differed from the Roman and native ones. In a sense, medieval history is the account of the synthesizing of these new elements with the old, under the stimulus of Christianity.*

✓   ✓   ✓

2. . . . The name Germany, on the other hand, they say, is modern and newly introduced, from the fact that the tribes which first crossed the Rhine and drove out the Gauls, and are now called Tungrians, were then called Germans. Thus what was the name of a tribe, and not of a race, gradually prevailed, till all called themselves by

---

[1] Alfred John Church and William Jackson Brodribb, trans., *The Complete Works of Tacitus* (New York, Random House, 1942), pp. 709-732, *passim.*

this self-invented name of Germans, which the conquerors had first employed to inspire terror. . . .

4. For my own part, I agree with those who think that the tribes of Germany are free from all taint of inter-marriages with foreign nations, and that they appear as a distinct, unmixed race, like none but themselves. Hence, too, the same physical peculiarities throughout so vast a population. All have fierce blue eyes, red hair, huge frames, fit only for a sudden exertion. They are less able to bear laborious work. Heat and thirst they cannot in the least endure; to cold and hunger their climate and their soil inure them. . . .

6. Even iron is not plentiful with them, as we infer from the character of their weapons. But few use swords or long lances. They carry a spear (*framea* is their name for it), with a narrow and short head, but so sharp and easy to wield that the same weapon serves, according to circumstances, for close or distant conflict. As for the horse-soldier, he is satisfied with a shield and spear; the foot-soldiers also scatter showers of missiles, each man having several and hurling them to an immense distance, and being naked or lightly clad with a little cloak. There is no display about their equipment: their shields alone are marked with very choice colours. A few only have corslets, and just one or two here and there a metal or leathern helmet. Their horses are remarkable neither for beauty nor for fleetness. . . .

7. They choose their kings by birth, their generals for merit. These kings have not unlimited or arbitrary power, and the generals do more by example than by authority. . . . They also carry with them into battle certain figures and images taken from their sacred groves. And what most stimulates their courage is, that their squadrons or battalions, instead of being formed by chance or by a fortuitous gathering, are composed of families and clans. Close by them, too, are those dearest to them, so that they hear the shrieks of women, the cries of infants. *They* are to every man the most sacred witness of his bravery—*they* are his most generous applauders. . . .

9. Mercury is the deity whom they chiefly worship, and on certain days they deem it right to sacrifice to him even

with human victims. Hercules and Mars they appease
with more lawful offerings. . . .

10. Augury and divination by lot no people practise
more diligently. The use of the lots is simple. A little
bough is lopped off a fruit-bearing tree, and cut into small
pieces; these are distinguished by certain marks, and
thrown carelessly and at random over a white garment.
In public questions the priest of the particular state, in
private the father of the family, invokes the gods, and,
with his eyes towards heaven, takes up each piece three
times, and finds in them a meaning according to the mark
previously impressed on them. . . .

11. About minor matters the chiefs deliberate, about
the more important the whole tribe. Yet even when the
final decision rests with the people, the affair is always
thoroughly discussed by the chiefs. They assemble, except
in the case of a sudden emergency, on certain fixed days,
either at new or at full moon; for this they consider the
most auspicious season for the transaction of business.
. . . When the multitude think proper, they sit down
armed. Silence is proclaimed by the priests, who have on
these occasions the right of keeping order. Then the king
or the chief, according to age, birth, distinction in war,
or eloquence, is heard, more because he has influence to
persuade than because he has power to command. If his
sentiments displease them, they reject them with mur-
murs; if they are satisfied, they brandish their spears. The
most complimentary form of assent is to express approbation with their weapons.

13. . . . Very noble birth or great services rendered by
the father secure for lads the rank of a chief; such lads
attach themselves to men of mature strength and of long
approved valour. It is no shame to be seen among a chief's
followers. . . .

15. Whenever they are not fighting, they pass much of
their time in the chase, and still more in idleness, giving
themselves up to sleep and to feasting, the bravest and
the most warlike doing nothing, and surrendering the
management of the household, of the home, and of the
land, to the women, the old men, and all the weakest
members of the family. . . .

21. It is a duty among them to adopt the feuds as well as the friendships of a father or a kinsman. These feuds are not implacable; even homicide is expiated by the payment of a certain number of cattle and of sheep, and the satisfaction is accepted by the entire family. . . .

22. . . . To pass an entire day and night in drinking disgraces no one. Their quarrels, as might be expected with intoxicated people, are seldom fought out with mere abuse, but commonly with wounds and bloodshed. Yet it is at their feasts that they generally consult on the reconciliation of enemies, on the forming of matrimonial alliances, on the choice of chiefs, finally even on peace and war, for they think that at no time is the mind more open to simplicity of purpose or more warmed to noble aspirations.

24. . . . Strangely enough they make games of hazard a serious occupation even when sober, and so venturesome are they about gaining or losing, that, when every other resource has failed, on the last and final throw they stake the freedom of their own persons. The loser goes into voluntary slavery. . . . Slaves of this kind the owners part with in the way of commerce, and also to relieve themselves from the scandal of such a victory.

25. The other slaves are not employed after our manner with distinct domestic duties assigned to them, but each one has the management of a house and home of his own. The master requires from the slave a certain quantity of grain, of cattle, and of clothing, as he would from a tenant, and this is the limit of subjection. . . .

33. . . . May the tribes, I pray, ever retain if not love for us, at least hatred for each other; for while the destinies of empire hurry us on, fortune can give no greater boon than discord among our foes.

— 2 —

THE EARLY CHRISTIAN CHURCH

The so-called Edict of Milan, issued in 313 by Constantine and Licinius, marked the official termination of the persecution of Christians except for the brief reign of Julian (361-363). The Emperor Nero had instituted the first persecution probably to divert suspicion from himself that he had set fire to Rome. Thereafter, Christians could not be certain when they would be subject to discrimination. The letter from the Christians at Lyons and Vienne is poignant testimony of what could happen in any city of the empire. It is not hard to understand that the strength of the Christians before their tormentors attracted many people to them. Early church writers were also concerned with the problem, and the passage from Tertullian reflects the opinions of one of the most learned.

It was not until 250 that a general persecution of Christians was launched by the emperor Decius, but the decree was mitigated the following year by his successor Valerian. The Christians refused to worship the emperor, met in secret, and so seemed to an empire undergoing civil wars, invasions, and other calamities to be practically subversive. The worst attack on them came toward the end of the third century in the reign of Diocletian. Shortly after the turn of the century a more tolerant atmosphere developed, and the Christians, although a minority, were officially tolerated in 313.

✦   ✦   ✦

A. THE PERSECUTION OF CHRISTIANS AT LYONS AND VIENNE, *ca.* 178[1]

[1] Eusebius, Ecclesiastical History, V, 1. Trans. A. C. McGiffert, *Nicene and Post-Nicene Fathers*, 2nd Ser., I, 212-217.

The following letter, from which extracts are given, was written to fellow Christians in Asia and Phrygia by an eye-witness.

✓   ✓   ✓

The greatness of the tribulation in this region, and the fury of the heathen against the saints, and the sufferings of the blessed witnesses, we cannot recount accurately, nor indeed could they possibly be recorded. For with all his might the adversary fell upon us, giving us a foretaste of his unbridled activity at his future coming. He endeavored in every manner to practice and exercise his servants against the servants of God, not only shutting us out from houses and baths and markets, but forbidding any of us to be seen in any place whatever. But the grace of God led the conflict against him, and delivered the weak, and set them as firm pillars, able through patience to endure all the wrath of the Evil One. And they joined battle with him, undergoing all kinds of shame and injury; and regarding their great sufferings as little, they hastened to Christ, manifesting truly that "the sufferings of this present time are not worthy to be compared with the glory which shall be revealed to us-ward." First of all, they endured nobly the injuries heaped upon them by the populace; clamors and blows and draggings and robberies and stonings and imprisonments, and all things which an infuriated mob delight in inflicting on enemies and adversaries. Then, being taken to the forum by the chiliarch and the authorities of the city, they were examined in the presence of the whole multitude, and having confessed, they were imprisoned until the arrival of the governor. . . .

But the whole wrath of the populace, and governor, and soldiers was aroused exceedingly against Sanctus, the deacon from Vienne, and Maturus, a late convert, yet a noble combatant, and against Attalus, a native of Pergamos, where he had always been a pillar and foundation, and Blandina, through whom Christ showed that things which appear mean and obscure and despicable to men are with God of great glory, through love toward him manifested in power, and not boasting in appearance. For while we all trembled, and her earthly mistress, who was herself also one of the witnesses, feared that on account of the weakness of her body, she would be unable to make bold confession, Blandina was filled with such power as to be delivered and raised above those who were torturing her by turns from morning till evening in every manner, so that they acknowledged that they were conquered, and could do nothing more to her. And they were astonished at her endurance, as her entire body was mangled and broken; and they testified that one of these forms of torture was sufficient to destroy life, not to speak of so many and so great sufferings. But the blessed woman, like a noble athlete, renewed her strength in her confession; and her comfort and recreation and relief from the pain of her sufferings was in exclaiming, "I am a Christian, and there is nothing vile done by us. . . ."

But Blandina was suspended on a stake, and exposed to be devoured by the wild beasts who should attack her. And because she appeared as if hanging on a cross, and because of her earnest prayers, she inspired the combatants with great zeal. For they looked on her in her conflict, and beheld with their outward eyes, in the form of their sister, him who was crucified for them, that he might persuade those who believe on him, that every one who suffers for the glory of Christ has fellowship always with the living God. As none of the wild beasts at that time touched her, she was taken down from the stake, and cast again into prison. She was preserved thus for another contest, that, being victorious in more conflicts, she might make the punishment of the crooked serpent irrevocable; and, though small and weak and despised, yet clothed with Christ the mighty and conquering Athlete, she might arouse the zeal of the brethren, and, having overcome the adversary many times might receive, through her conflict, the crown incorruptible. . . .

The bodies of the martyrs, having thus in every manner been exhibited and exposed for six days, were afterward burned and reduced to ashes, and swept into the Rhone by the wicked men, so that no trace of them might appear on the earth. And this they did, as if able to conquer God, and prevent their new birth; "that," as they said, "they may have no hope of a resurrection, through trust in which they bring to us this foreign and new religion, and despise terrible things, and are ready even to go to death with joy. Now let us see if they will rise again, and if their God is able to help them, and to deliver them out of our hands."

B. TERTULLIAN ON PERSECUTION, *ca.* 208 [1]

The question in hand is persecution. With respect to this, let me in the meantime say, that nothing happens without God's will; on the ground that persecution is especially worthy of God, and, so to speak, requisite, for the approving, to wit, or if you will, the rejection of His professing servants. For what is the issue of persecution, what other result comes of it, but the approving and rejection of faith, in regard to which the Lord will certainly sift His people? Persecution, by means of which one is declared either approved or rejected, is just the judgment of the Lord. . . . So, too, persecution may be viewed as a contest. By whom is the conflict proclaimed, but by Him by whom the crown and the rewards are offered? . . . The one great thing in persecution is the promotion of the glory of God, as He tries and casts away, lays on and takes off. . . .

C. THE LAST PERSECUTION OF CHRISTIANS, 303 [2]

It was in the nineteenth year of the reign of Diocletian, in the month Dystrus, called March by the Romans, when the feast of the Saviour's passion was near at hand, that royal edicts were published everywhere, commanding that the churches be leveled to the ground, and the Scriptures be destroyed by fire, and ordering that those who held places of honor be degraded, and that the household servants, if they persisted in the profession of Christianity, be deprived of freedom.

[1] Tertullian, *De fuga in persecutione*, Ch. 1, trans. S. Thelwall, *Ante-Nicene Fathers*, IV, 116-117.

[2] Eusebius, Ecclesiastical History, VIII, 2, trans. A. C. McGiffert, *Nicene and Post-Nicene Fathers*, 2nd Ser., I, 324.

D. THE EDICT OF MILAN, 313 [1]

When I, Constantine Augustus, as well as I, Licinius Augustus, had fortunately met near Mediolanum [Milan], and were considering everything that pertained to the public welfare and security, we thought that, among other things which we saw would be for the good of many, those regulations pertaining to the reverence of the Divinity ought certainly to be made first, so that we might grant to the Christians and to all others full authority to ob-serve that religion which each preferred; whence any Divinity whatsoever in the seat of the heavens may be propitious and kindly disposed to us and all who are placed under our rule. And thus by this wholesome counsel and most upright provision we thought to arrange that no one whatsoever should be denied the opportunity to give his heart to the observance of the Christian reli-gion, or of that religion which he should think best for himself, so that the supreme Deity, to whose worship we freely yield our hearts, may show in all things His usual favor and benevolence. Therefore, your Worship should know that it has pleased us to remove all conditions what-soever, which were in the rescripts formerly given to you officially, concerning the Christians, and now any one of these who wishes to observe the Christian religion may do so freely and openly, without any disturbance or molestation. We thought it fit to commend these things most fully to your care that you may know that we have given to those Christians free and unrestricted oppor-tunity of religious worship. When you see that this has been granted to them by us, your Worship will know that we have also conceded to other religions the right of open and free observance of their worship for the sake of the peace of our times, that each one may have the free op-portunity to worship as he pleases; this regulation is made that we may not seem to detract aught from any dignity or any religion. Moreover, in the case of the Christians especially, we esteemed it best to order that if

[1] University of Pennsylvania, "Translations and Reprints" (Philadelphia, 1897), IV, 1, 29-30. Cited hereafter as Univ. of Penn., "Trans. and Rep."

it happens that anyone heretofore has bought from our treasury or from anyone whatsoever, those places where they were previously accustomed to assemble, concerning which a certain decree had been made and a letter sent to you officially, the same shall be restored to the Christians without payment or any claim of recompense and without any kind of fraud or deception. Those, moreover, who have obtained the same by gift, are likewise to return them at once to the Christians. Besides, both those who have purchased and those who have secured them by gift, are to appeal to the vicar if they seek any recompense from our bounty, that they may be cared for through our clemency. All this property ought to be delivered at once to the community of the Christians through your intercession, and without delay. And since these Christians are known to have possessed not only those places in which they were accustomed to assemble, but also other property, namely the churches, belonging to them as a corporation and not as individuals, all these things which we have included under the above law, you will order to be restored, without any hesitation or controversy at all, to these Christians, that is to say to the corporations and their conventicles :- providing, of course, that the above arrangements be followed so that those who return the same without payment, as we have said, may hope for an indemnity from our bounty. In all these circumstances you ought to tender your most efficacious intervention to the community of the Christians, that our command may be carried into effect as quickly as possible, whereby, moreover, through our clemency, public order may be secured. Let this be done so that, as we have said above, Divine favor towards us, which, under the most important circumstances we have already experienced, may, for all time, preserve and prosper our successes together with the good of the state. Moreover, in order that the statement of this decree of our good will may come to the notice of all, this rescript, published by your decree, shall be announced everywhere and brought to the knowledge of all, so that the decree of this, our benevolence, cannot be concealed.

— 3 —

AN EDICT OF THE EMPEROR THEODOSIUS AGAINST HERETICS, 425[1]

This is an example of the many imperial edicts against heretics issued in the century following the Council of Nicea in 325.

✓ ✓ ✓

We command that the Manichaeans, heretics, schismatics, astrologers, and every sect inimical to the Catholics shall be banished from the very sight of the City of Rome, in order that it may not be contaminated by the contagious presence of the criminals. An admonition, moreover, must be especially issued concerning those persons who by perverse persuasion withdraw from the communion of the venerable Pope, and by whose schism the rest of the common people also are corrupted. By the issuance of this notification We grant to them a truce of twenty days. Unless they return within that time to the unity of communion, they shall be expelled from the City as far as the hundredth milestone and shall be tormented by the solitude of their own choice.

[1] *The Theodosian Code,* XVI. 5. 62, trans. Clyde Pharr (Princeton University Press, 1952), p. 462.

— 4 —

CASSIODORUS DESCRIBES THE PRINCIPLES OF HIS ADMINISTRATION, *ca.* 535 [1]

Theodoric, king of the Ostrogoths (493-526), is perhaps the most attractive of the so-called barbarian kings. Having led his people into Italy, which was easily conquered, he inaugurated a tolerant and wise reign. One of his principal ministers was Cassiodorus (ca. 480-ca. 575), a member of an old aristocratic family. He continued in high office under Theodoric's successors and finally retired about 540 to found two monasteries on his ancestral estates, where he continued to write. But his importance in this new life is that he instituted as a regular part of the monastic routine the copying and binding of manuscripts. He was, in effect, the originator of the scriptorium, *which was to be an integral part of future monasteries and the means through which much classical and all Christian writings were to be copied and transmitted. The following edict to the provinces written on his accession as Praetorian Prefect, besides indicating his administrative principles, also presents an insight into Cassiodorus' character as a high official of a barbarian.*

✓   ✓   ✓

The custom of the ancients was for a new ruler to promulgate a new set of laws to his subjects, but now it is sufficient praise to a conscientious ruler that he adheres to the legislation of Antiquity.

Do you all study to perform good actions, and shrink from deeds of lawlessness and sedition, and you will have

[1] Thomas Hodgkin, *The Letters of Cassiodorus* (London, 1886), pp. 465-467.

nothing to fear from your Governors. I know that some fear, however irrational, is felt in the presence of the Judge; but as far as my purpose can avail, with the help of God and the rulers of the State, I can promise you that all things shall be done with justice and moderation.

Venality, that greatest stain upon a Judge's character, will be unknown in me; for I should think scorn to sell the words that go out of my lips, like clothes in the market-place.

In exercising the right of pre-emption we shall be solely guided by the wants of the State, buying nothing at a forced price in order to sell it again.

Be cheerful and of good courage, therefore, with reference to the new administration. No soldier or civil servant shall harass you for his own pleasure. No tax-collector shall load you with burdens of his own imposition. We are determined to keep not only our own hands clean, but also those of our officials. Otherwise, vainly does a good Judge guard himself from receiving money, if he leaves to the many under him licence to receive it on their own account. But we, both by precept and example, show that we aim at the public good, not at private and fraudulent gains.

We know what prayers you put up for us, how anxiously you watched for our elevation, and we are determined that you shall not be disappointed. Our Praetorium, which no base action has ever defiled, shall be open to all. No servile throng shall lord it over you. You shall come straight to us, making your requests known to us through no hired interpreter, and none shall leave our presence poorer than he entered it. With God's help we trust we shall so act as to conform to the instructions which we have received from our Sovereign; and we trust that you, by your loyalty, will enable us to be rather the Father of our Provinces than their Judge. You have patiently obeyed governors who fleeced you; how much more ought you to obey one who, as you know, loves you mightily! Pay the regular fees to the officials who are laboring in your midst; for there is no such excuse for high-handed oppression as the fact that a man is not receiving his covenanted salary. Obey the rule of reason, and you will not have to fear the armed man's wrath.

We wish that you should enjoy the privileges conceded to you by former rulers without any encroachment by violent men.

And now be of good heart; I pledge myself for your righteous government. Had I been present with you face to face, ye could not have seen my mind; but ye can read it in this letter, which is the mirror of my heart, the true image of my will, and ye can see that it desires only your prosperity.

— 5 —

AN EARLY CHRISTIAN VIEW OF THE UNIVERSE, ca. 547[1]

A principal enemy of the Christians was paganism and its literature. About 547 a monk called Cosmas wrote The Christian Topography *which provided a refutation of pagan geography and put in its place one based on holy writ. Extracts from his book are given below. Much of Cosmas' book was useful and reliable because he had visited many of the places he describes as a trader, but much else was fanciful.*

1   1   1

We have said that the figure of the earth is lengthwise from east to west, and breadthwise from north to south, and that it is divided into two parts: this part which we, the men of the present day, inhabit, and which is all round encircled by the intermedial sea, called the ocean by the Pagans, and that part which encircles the ocean, and has

[1] Cosmas, *The Christian Topography,* trans. J. W. McCrindle, (The Hakluyt Society, London, 1897), *passim.*

its extremities bound together with those of the heaven, and which men at one time inhabited to eastward, before the flood in the days of Noah occurred, and in which also Paradise is situated. . . .

The northern and western parts of the earth which we inhabit are of very great elevation, while the southern parts are proportionately depressed. For to what extent of its breadth the earth is imperceptibly depressed, it is found to have an elevation of like area in the northern and western parts, while the ocean beyond is of unusual depth. But in the southern and eastern parts the ocean beyond is not of unusual but of the medium depth. When these facts are considered, one can see why those who sail to the north and the west are called lingerers. It is because they are mounting up and in mounting up they sail more slowly, while in returning they descend from high places to low, and thus sail fast, and in a few days bring their voyage to an end. . . . The eastern and southern parts again, as low-lying and over-heated by the sun, are extremely hot, while the northern and western from their great elevation and distance from the sun are extremely cold, and in consequence the inhabitants have very pale complexions, and must keep themselves warm against the cold. . . .

Since then the heaven and the earth comprise the universe, we assert that the earth has been founded on its own stability by the Creator, according once more to the divine scripture, and that it does not rest on any body. . . . We therefore first depict along with the earth the heaven, which is vaulted and which has its extremities bound together with the extremities of the earth. To the best of our ability we have endeavoured to delineate it on its western side and its eastern; for these two sides are walls, extending from below to the vault above. There is also the firmament which, in the middle, is bound together with the first heaven, and which, on its upper side, has the waters according to divine scripture itself. . . . To the extremities on the four sides of the earth the heaven is fastened at its own four extremities, making the figure of a cube, that is to say, a quadrangular figure, while up above it curves round in the form of an oblong vault and becomes as it were a vast canopy. And in the middle the firmament is made fast to it, and thus two places are formed.

From the earth to the firmament is the first place, this world, namely, in which are the angels and men and all the present state of existence. From the firmament again to the vault above is the second place—the Kingdom of Heaven, into which Christ, first of all, entered, after his ascension, having prepared for us a new and living way. . . .

Since the heavenly bodies then, according to divine scripture, are moved in their orbits by invisible powers, and run their course through the north, and pass below the elevated part of the earth, it is possible, with such a configuration, for eclipses of the moon and the sun to be produced. For the angelic powers, by moving the figures on rational principles and in regular order, and with greater speed than lies in us to apprehend, produce these phenomena, plying their labors by night and by day without ever pausing. . . .

— 6 —

THE ORGANIZATION OF THE ENGLISH CHURCH, 601 [1]

The following letter to Augustine, the missionary to England, from Pope Gregory I, informs him how to organize the new church. Gregory's idea of two metropolitans, in the north and south, was carried out, but Canterbury never agreed to cede its position to London as the pope suggests should be done.

[1] Epistles of Gregory the Great, Epistle LXV, trans. James Barmby, in *Nicene and Post-Nicene Fathers,* 2nd Ser., XIII, p. 81.

Gregory to Augustine, etc.

Though it is certain that for those who labor for Almighty God ineffable rewards of an eternal kingdom are reserved, yet we must needs bestow honors upon them, that by reason of remuneration they may apply themselves the more manifoldly in devotion to spiritual work. And, since the new Church of the Angli has been brought to the grace of Almighty God through the bountifulness of the same Lord and thy labors, we grant to thee the use of the pallium therein for the solemnization of mass only, so that thou mayest ordain bishops in twelve several places, to be subject to thy jurisdiction, with the view of a bishop of the city of London being always consecrated in future by his own synod, and receiving the dignity of the pallium from this holy and Apostolical See which by the grace of God I serve. Further, to the city of York we desire thee to send a bishop whom thou mayest judge fit to be ordained; so that, if this same city with the neighboring places should receive the word of God, he also may ordain twelve bishops, so as to enjoy the dignity of a metropolitan: for to him also, if our life is continued, we propose, with the favor of God, to send a pallium; but yet we desire to subject him to the control of thy Fraternity. But after thy death let him be over the bishops whom he shall have ordained, so as to be in no wise subject to the jurisdiction of the bishop of London. Further, between the bishops of London and York in the future let there be this distinction of dignity, that he be accounted first who has been first ordained. But let them arrange by council in common, and with concordant action, whatever things may have to be done in zeal for Christ; let them be of one mind in what is right, and accomplish what they are minded to do without disagreement with each other.

But let thy Fraternity have subject to thyself under our God not only those bishops whom thou shalt ordain, and those whom the bishop of York may ordain, but also all the priests of Britain, to the end that they may learn the form of right belief and good living from the tongue and life of thy Holiness, and, executing their office well in their faith and manners, may attain to heavenly kingdoms when it may please the Lord. God keep thee safe, most reverend brother. Given on the tenth day of the Kalends of July, in the 19th year of the empire of our lord Mauricius Tiberius, the 18th year after the consulship of the same lord, Indiction 4.

— 7 —

THE CORONATION OF CHARLEMAGNE, DECEMBER 25, 800[1]

Charlemagne arrived in Rome November 23, 800 to hear complaints against Pope Leo III, which he dismissed in due course. The event described below marks the culmination of the relationship that had been developing between the papacy and the Frankish kings for fifty years. It is also the start of a new axis, Roman pope and German emperor, that would be a central fact in medieval history. Leo's act was technically illegal because there was already a Roman emperor at Constantinople, albeit a woman named Irene. But reality overcame legality, and Charlemagne was recognized as emperor by the Eastern emperor, Michael, in 813.

✓   ✓   ✓

On the most holy day of the birth of our Lord [the king came to mass in the basilica of the blessed apostle Peter]. Pope Leo placed a crown on his head and joined by all the Romans proclaimed, "Long life and victory to

[1] *Ann. reg. Francorum,* as printed in Robert Latouche, *Textes d'histoire médiévale* (Paris, 1951), p. 115.

Charles Augustus crowned by God, the great and pacific Emperor of the Romans." And after this proclamation by the pope he bowed humbly to him as was the custom in ancient times and he discarded the title of patrician and was addressed as emperor and Augustus.

— 8 —

MILITARY SERVICE UNDER CHARLEMAGNE, ca. 800[1]

Charlemagne's constant military campaigns required a considerable amount of organization. A number of the capitularies he issued on the subject have survived and extracts are given from a few of them.

✓   ✓   ✓

Capitulare Haristallense, 779

Ch. 14. Let no one presume to gather an armed following (*truste*).

Ch. 20. Let no one dare to sell any byrnies [coats of mail] outside of our realm.

Capitulare Italicum, 801

Ch. 3. Concerning deserters. If anyone shall have shown himself so contumacious or haughty as to leave the army and return home without the command or permission of the king, that is, if he is guilty of what we call in the German language *herisliz*, he himself, as a criminal, shall incur the peril of losing his life, and his property shall be confiscated for our treasury.

[1] Univ. of Penn., "Trans. and Rep.," VI, 5, 6-11, *passim*.

*Capitulare missorum in Theodonis Villa
datum secundum, generale,* 805 (?)

Ch. 6. Concerning the equipment in the army the same
shall be observed as we have previously commanded in
another [lost] capitulary, and, in particular, every man
who possesses twelve *mansi* shall have a byrnie; he who
has a byrnie and shall not have brought it with him shall
lose his whole benefice, together with the byrnie.

Capitulare missorum de exercitu promovendo, 808

Ch. 1. Every free man who has four *mansi* of his own
property, or as a benefice from anyone, shall equip himself and go to the army, either with his lord, if the lord
goes, or with his count. He who has three *mansi* of his
own property shall be joined to a man who has one
mansus, and shall aid him so that he may serve for both.
He who has only two *mansi* of his own property shall be
joined to another who likewise has two *mansi,* and one of
them, with the aid of the other, shall go to the army. He
who has only one *mansus* of his own shall be joined to
one of three who have the same and shall aid him, and
the latter shall go alone; the three who have aided him
shall remain at home.

Ch. 4. From the men who have been enfeoffed by the
counts the following are to be excepted and are not commanded to pay the ban: two who shall have been left
behind with the wife of a count and two others who shall
have been commanded to remain to guard his territory
and to perform our service. In this case we command,
however, that each count shall leave at home two men to
guard each separate territory which he has, in addition
to those two who remain with his wife; all the others,
without any exception, he shall have with him, or if he
remains at home, he shall order them to proceed with the
one who goes to the army in his stead. A bishop or abbot
shall leave at home only two of those who are enfeoffed
and laymen.

Capitulare Bononiense, October, 811

Ch. 3. If any man holding an office under us shall have
been summoned to the host and shall not have come to

the appointed muster, he shall abstain from flesh and wine
for as many days as he shall have been proved to be late
in coming to the appointed muster.

Ch. 6. That in the host no one shall ask his peer or any
other man to drink. And if any drunken person shall have
been found in the army, he shall be so excommunicated
that in drinking he shall use nothing but water until he
acknowledges that he has acted wrongly.

Ch. 8. It has been enacted that the preparation for
serving in the army shall be defined and continued in
accordance with the ancient custom, namely, victuals for
a three months' march and arms and clothing for a half-
year. . . .

Capitulare Aquisgranense, 801-813

Ch. 10. That the equipments of the king shall be carried
in carts, also the equipments of the bishops, counts, abbots
and nobles of the king; flour, wine, pork and victuals in
abundance, mills, adzes, axes, augers, slings, and men
who know how to use these well. And the marshals of the
king shall add stones for these on twenty beasts of burden, if there is need. And each one shall be prepared for
the army and shall have plenty of all utensils. And each
count shall save two parts of the fodder in his county for
the army's use, and he shall have good bridges, good
boats.

— 9 —

AN INVENTORY OF AN ESTATE OF CHARLEMAGNE, ca. 800[1]

Charlemagne's administrative capacity is revealed by his capitularies, which cover a wide range of interests from education to routine instructions to officials. The capitulary De Villis *instructs the stewards of his estates to forward to him an annual inventory of the estate entrusted to them. The following is an example of one such report. It is easy to imagine the daily routine and living conditions on this estate, but unfortunately its location is not known.*

✓   ✓   ✓

We found in the domain estate of Asnapium a royal house built of stone in the best manner, 3 rooms; the whole house surrounded with balconies, with 11 apartments for women; beneath 1 cellar; 2 porticoes; 17 other houses built of wood within the court-yard with as many rooms and other appurtenances, well built; 1 stable, 1 kitchen, 1 mill, 1 granary, 3 barns.

The yard surrounded carefully with a hedge and stone gateway and above a balcony from which to make distributions. An inner yard, likewise enclosed within a hedge, arranged in a suitable manner planted with various kinds of trees.

Vestments: coverings for 1 bed, 1 table cloth, 1 towel.

Utensils: 2 brass kettles, 2 drinking cups, 2 brass cauldrons, 1 iron one, 1 frying-pan, 1 gramalmin, 1 pair of andirons, 1 lamp, 2 hatchets, 1 chisel, 2 augers, 1 axe, 1 knife, 1 large plane, 1 plane, 2 scythes, 2 sickles, 2 spades tipped with iron. Enough wooden utensils for use.

Farm produce: old spelt from last year, 90 baskets

which can be made into 450 weight of flour; 100 measures
of barley. From the present year, 110 baskets of spelt,
planted 60 baskets from the same, the rest we found; 100
measures of wheat, 60 sown, the rest we found; 98 measures of rye all sown; 1800 measures of barley, 1100 sown,
the rest we found; 430 measures of oats, 1 measure of
beans, 12 measures of peas. At the 5 mills, 800 measures,
small measures. At the 4 breweries, 650 measures, small
measures, 240 given to the prebendaries, the rest we
found. At the 2 bridges, 60 measures of salt and 2 shillings. At the 4 gardens, 11 shillings. Honey, 3 measures;
about 1 measure of butter; lard, from last year 10 sides,
new sides 200 with fragments and fats, cheese from the
present year 43 weights.

Of cattle; 51 head of larger cattle, 5 three-year-olds, 7
two-year-olds, 7 yearlings; 10 two-year-old colts, 8 yearlings, 3 stallions; 16 cows; 2 asses; 50 cows with calves,
20 young bullocks, 38 yearling calves, 3 bulls, 260 hogs,
100 pigs, 5 boars, 150 sheep with lambs, 200 yearling
lambs, 120 rams, 30 goats with kids, 30 yearling kids,
3 male goats, 30 geese, 80 chickens, 22 peacocks.

Also concerning the dependencies which pertain to the
above mansion. In the villa of Grisio we found domain
buildings, where there are 3 barns and a yard surrounded
by a hedge. There is there 1 garden with trees, 10 geese,
8 ducks, 30 chickens.

In another villa. We found domain buildings and a yard
surrounded by a hedge and within 3 barns, 1 arpent of
vines, 1 garden with trees, 15 geese, 20 chickens.

In a third villa, domain buildings. It has 2 barns, 1
granary, 1 garden, 1 yard well enclosed by a hedge.

We found all the dry and liquid measures just as in the
palace. We did not find any goldsmiths, silversmiths,
blacksmiths, huntsmen or persons engaged in other services.

The garden herbs which we found were lily, putchuck,
mint, parsley, rue, celery, *libesticum,* sage, savory, juni-
per, leeks, garlic, tansy, wild mint, coriander, scallions,
onions, cabbage, kohl-rabi, betony Trees: pears, apples,
medlars, peaches, filberts, walnuts, mulberries, quinces.

— 10 —

THE REVIVAL OF LEARNING
UNDER CHARLEMAGNE, *ca.* 800[1]

*Charlemagne's interest in education, including his own,
is well known. An active group of intellectuals was housed
at his court, but as the extracts from several letters show,
he was also concerned with learning throughout his empire.*

Letter of Charlemagne to Abbot Baugulf, 780-800

(Greetings.) Be it known, therefore, to your devotion
pleasing to God, that we, together with our faithful, have
considered it to be useful that the bishoprics and monasteries entrusted by the favor of Christ to our control, in
addition to the order of monastic life and the intercourse
of holy religion, in the culture of letters also ought to be
zealous in teaching those who by the gift of God are able
to learn, according to the capacity of each individual, so
that just as the observance of the rule imparts order and
grace to honesty of morals, so also zeal in teaching and
learning may do the same for sentences, so that those who
desire to please God by living rightly should not neglect
to please him also by speaking correctly. . . . For although correct conduct may be better than knowledge,
nevertheless knowledge precedes conduct. . . . For when
in the years just passed letters were often written to us
from several monasteries in which it was stated that the
brethren who dwelt there offered up in our behalf sacred
and pious prayers, we have recognized in most of these
letters both correct thoughts and uncouth expressions;

[1] Univ. of Penn., "Trans. and Rep.," VI, 5, 12-15, *passim.*

because what pious devotion dictated faithfully to the mind, the tongue, uneducated on account of the neglect of study, was not able to express in the letter without error. . . . Therefore, we exhort you not only not to neglect the study of letters, but also with most humble mind, pleasing to God, to study earnestly in order that you may be able more easily and more correctly to penetrate the mysteries of the divine Scriptures. . . .

Letter of Charlemagne to the religious lectors, 786-800

. . . Therefore, because we take care constantly to improve the condition of our churches, we have striven with watchful zeal to advance the cause of learning, which has been almost forgotten by the negligence of our ancestors; and, by our example, also we invite those whom we can to master the study of the liberal arts. Accordingly, God aiding us in all things, we have already corrected carefully all the books of the Old and New Testaments, corrupted by the ignorance of the copyists.

Incited, moreover, by the example of our father Pippin, of venerated memory, who by his zeal decorated all the churches of the Gauls with the songs of the Roman church, we are careful by our skill to make these churches illustrious by a series of excellent lectionaries. Finally, because we have found the lectionaries for the nocturnal offices, compiled by the fruitless labor of certain ones, in spite of their correct intention, unsuitable because they were written without the words of their authors and were full of an infinite number of errors, we cannot suffer in our days discordant solecisms to glide into the sacred lessons among the holy offices, and we purpose to improve these lessons. . . .

Letter of Charlemagne, 789

. . . and let them (ministers) join and associate to themselves not only children of servile condition, but also sons of free men. And let schools be established in which boys may learn to read. . . .

— 11 —

THE STRASBOURG OATHS, 842[1]

Charlemagne's only surviving legitimate son, King Louis I the Pious, divided the empire among his three sons—Lothair, Pepin, and Louis—in 817. By a second marriage Louis I had another son, Charles, and he was awarded lands from those held by his half-brothers. A series of rebellions followed, and when Pepin died his sons continued his cause. The death of Louis I in 840 was scarcely noticed by his sons as they continued their quarreling. Lothair, who had succeeded to the imperial title and wished to rule his brothers, thereby forced Charles and Louis to join forces in opposition and take the following oaths on February 14, 842. Two points are of interest: the kings did not break their vows immediately, and each took the oath in the language of the other; Charles who ruled the western third of the empire spoke it in German, Louis who ruled an accumulation of eastern lands that are conveniently called Germany, spoke a Romance language that would eventually become French. The following year, after invading Lothair's kingdom, they agreed to the Treaty of Verdun which "laid out the general lines of the national development of Western Europe."

ƒ   ƒ   ƒ

Charles and Louis each swore before the other's troops: For the love of God and Christian people and our mutual salvation, from this day forward, as far as God gives me knowledge and power, I will come to the assistance of this my brother Charles (Louis) with my aid and in every

[1] Nithard, *Histoire des fils de Louis le Pieux* (*Les Classiques de l'histoire de France au Moyen Age* (Paris, 1926), pp. 104-108.

affair, as one ought to help his brother, providing he
does likewise for me, and I will never take Lothair's side
in any cause, which by my act could be harmful to my
brother Charles (Louis).

*The troops of each monarch then swore the following
in their own tongue:*

If Louis (Charles) keeps the oath he has sworn to his
brother Charles (Louis) and Charles (Louis) my lord,
does not keep it on his part, if I cannot dissuade him
from it, neither I nor any of those that I am able to divert
from him will ever be of any help to him against Louis
(Charles).

— 12 —

THE TREATY OF VERDUN, 843[1]

*The three sons of Louis the Pious—Lothair, Louis the
German, and Charles the Bald—agreed to divide the empire between them. The agreement of 843 is brief by our
standards, considering especially what we know were to
be the consequences, but the vast amount of work that
went into it is hinted at by the first selection from the
preceding year. Bearing in mind the languages used by
Louis and Charles for the Strasbourg Oaths and the
fate that befell Lothair's kingdom by the end of the ninth
century, the Treaty of Verdun may be considered to be of
the first importance in the political history of Europe.*

842

Charles left Metz in October to go to Worms and join
his brother Louis. They remained there a long time and

---

[1] *Annales Bertiniani,* as printed in Latouche, *Textes d'histoire
médiévale* (Paris, 1951), pp. 126-128.

missi visited Lothair and they spent many days consulting on the division of the kingdom. Finally they decided to send diligent *missi* throughout the entire area under their rule to make an accurate description which would provide for an absolutely equal division of the kingdoms. . . .

843

Charles went to meet his brothers at Verdun, and there they divided the kingdoms. Louis obtained everything beyond the Rhine and the cities and districts of Speier, Worms and Mainz on this side of the river; Lothair the land lying between the Rhine and the mouth of the Scheldt, Cambrai, Hainault, Lomme, Mézières and those counties which are contiguous to the Meuse on this side of the river to the confluence of the Saône and the Rhône, thence down the Rhône to the sea, together with the counties lying on both sides of the river; he received Artois outside of these boundaries because of the kindness of his brother Charles. All the rest of the land as far as Spain was granted to Charles. Having sworn oaths, each decamped and went to his land.

— 13 —

THE BEGINNINGS OF RUSSIA, *ca.* 860[1]

What must be considered the legendary origin and naming of Russia appears in the following passage. It is known, however, that the Russ raided Constantinople in 860. The Viking expansion of this period is a fact, and

[1] *The Russian Primary Chronicle*, as trans. by S. H. Cross and Sherbowitz-Wetzor (Mediaeval Academy of America), pp. 59-60.

it is probable that Swedes sailed eastward across the Baltic to Novgorod, and thence down the Dnieper River to Kiev.

✓ ✓ ✓

(860-862) The tributaries of the Varangians drove them back beyond the sea and, refusing them further tribute, set out to govern themselves. There was no law among them, but tribe rose against tribe. Discord thus ensued among them, and they began to war one against another. They said to themselves, "Let us seek a prince who may rule over us and judge us according to the Law." They accordingly went overseas to the Varangian Russes: these particular Varangians were known as Russes, just as some are called Swedes, and others Normans, English, and Gotlanders, for they were thus named. The Chuds, the Slavs, the Krivichians, and the Ves' then said to the people of Rus', "Our land is great and rich, but there is no order in it. Come to rule and reign over us." They thus selected three brothers, with their kinsfolk, who took with them all the Russes and migrated. The oldest, Rurik, located himself in Novgorod; the second, Sineus, at Beloozero; and the third, Truvor, in Izborsk. On account of these Varangians, the district of Novgorod became known as the land of Rus'. The present inhabitants of Novgorod are descended from the Varangian race, but aforetime they were Slavs.

— 14 —

THE SWEDES AND RUSSIA, 922 [1]

As part of the general expansion of Scandinavian peoples in the ninth century, the Swedes sailed down the rivers of western Russia. They established the Russian state based on Kiev, and by their contacts with the Byzantine and Moslem empires developed a wealthy and cosmopolitan realm. They were active traders, as the quantity of Arabic and Greek gold coins found in Sweden indicates. The following account is by a Moslem sent out from Baghdad by the caliph Al-Muktadir (908-932).

✓   ✓   ✓

I saw how the Northmen had arrived with their wares, and pitched their camp beside the Volga. Never did I see people so gigantic; they are as tall as palm trees; and florid and ruddy of complexion. They wear neither camisoles nor *chaftans,* but the men among them wear a garment of rough cloth, which is thrown over one side, so that one hand remains free. Every one carries an axe, a dagger, and a sword, and without these weapons they are never seen. Their swords are broad, with wavy lines, and of Frankish make. From the tip of the finger-nails to the neck, each man of them is tattooed with pictures of trees, living beings, and other things. The women carry, fastened to their breast, a little case of iron, copper, silver, or gold, according to the wealth and resources of their husbands. Fastened to the case they wear a ring, and upon that a dagger, all attached to their breast. About their necks they wear gold and silver chains. . . .

[A detailed account follows of the customs at a Norse

[1] Yākūt, *Geographical Dictionary,* as edited by Henry Goddard Leach, *A Pageant of Old Scandinavia* (Princeton, 1946), pp. 299-301.

funeral, culminating in the cremation of the body.] The
pile was soon aflame, then the ship, finally the tent, the
man, and the girl, and everything else in the ship. A
terrible storm began to blow up, and thus intensified the
flames, and gave wings to the blaze.

At my side stood one of the Northmen, and I heard
him talking with the interpreter, who stood near him. I
asked the interpreter what the Northman had said, and
received this answer: "You Arabs," he said, "must be a
stupid set! You take him who is to you the most revered
and beloved of men, and cast him to the ground, to be
devoured by creeping things and worms. We, on the
other hand, burn him in a twinkling, so that he instantly,
without a moment's delay, enters into Paradise." At this
he burst into uncontrollable laughter, and then continued,
"It is the love of the Master (God) that causes the wind
to blow and snatch him away in an instant." . . .

Thereupon they heaped over the place where the ship
had stood something like a rounded hill, and, erecting on
the centre of it a large birchen post, wrote on it the name
of the deceased, along with that of the king of the Northmen. Having done this, they left the spot.

— 15 —

THE TREATY BETWEEN ALFRED AND GUTHRUM, ca. 886[1]

*The Danes raided England for the first time at the
beginning of the ninth century. By the middle of the
century, especially after 855 when they spent the winter*

[1] F. L. Attenborough, ed. and trans., *The Laws of the Earliest
English Kings* (Cambridge University Press, 1922), pp.
99-101.

*in England, the raids are more accurately described as an
invasion. A particularly disastrous invasion in 866 was
to lead to the Danish capture of all seven kingdoms of
England but Wessex. The tide turned when King Alfred
of Wessex defeated the Danish king Guthrum in 878. The
latter accepted Christianity and withdrew to the area
thereafter called the Danelaw. The following treaty,
whose date is not exactly known, between the two kings
was evidently made after Alfred had reconquered more
lands from the Danes, including London. One result of
importance was that Alfred was recognized by the English outside the Danelaw as their king, and with him is
the genesis of English political unity.*

✓   ✓   ✓

These are the terms of peace which King Alfred and
King Guthrum, and the councillors of all the English
nation, and all the people who dwell in East Anglia, have
all agreed upon and confirmed with oaths, on their own
behalf and for their subjects, both living and unborn, who
are anxious for God's favor and ours.

1. First as to the boundaries between us. [They shall
run] up the Thames, and then up the Lea, and along the
Lea to its source, then in a straight line to Bedford, and
then up the Ouse to Watling Street.

2. Secondly, if a man is slain, whether he is an Englishman or a Dane, all of us shall place the same value
on his life—namely 8 half-marks of pure gold, with the
exception of commoners who occupy tributary land, and
freedmen of the Danes. These also shall be valued at the
same amount—(namely) 200 shillings—in either case.

3. If anyone accuses a king's thegn of homicide, if he
dares to clear himself, he shall do so with [the oaths of]
twelve king's thegns. If anyone accuses a man who belongs to a lower order than that of king's thegn, he shall
clear himself with [the oaths of] eleven of his equals and
one king's thegn. And this law shall apply to every suit
which involves an amount greater than 4 mancuses. And
if he [the accused] dare not [attempt to clear himself],
he shall pay [as compensation] three times the amount
at which the stolen property is valued.

4. Every man shall have knowledge of his warrantor when he buys slaves, or horses, or oxen.

5. And we all declared, on the day when the oaths were sworn, that neither slaves nor freemen should be allowed to pass over to the Danish host without permission, any more than that any of them [should come over] to us. If, however, it happens that any of them, in order to satisfy their wants, wish to trade with us, or we (for the same reason wish to trade) with them, in cattle and in goods, it shall be allowed on condition that hostages are given as security for peaceful behavior, and as evidence by which it may be known that no treachery is intended.

— 16 —

NORSE SEA ADVENTURES, ca. 1000 [1]

The destruction that the Norse and Danes wrought on Europe and England was enormous. But it must be admitted that they were singularly daring sailors and competent navigators, as their sailings across the North Atlantic Ocean testify. They settled in Iceland about 874, the same decade that saw other Norsemen ravage the Low Countries. About 986 some settled in Greenland, and about 1000 Leif Eriksson found Vinland the Good, as described below. From other sources that describe Vinland, some have suggested that Leif had blundered into Cape Cod. This may be the case, but it is clear that the Norse made no attempt to establish a permanent colony.

✓   ✓   ✓

[1] Snorri Sturluson, *Ólafs saga Tryggvasonar,* as edited by Henry Goddard Leach in *A Pageant of Old Scandinavia* (Princeton, 1946), p. 284.

That same summer the King [Olaf Tryggvason, 995-
1000] sent Gizur and Hjalti to Iceland, as has already
been written. At that time he also sent Leif Ericsson to
Greenland to preach Christianity there. The King sent
with him a priest and some other holy men to baptize the
people there, and to teach them the true faith. Leif went
to Greenland that same summer. He took on the sea [on
board his vessel] a ship's crew, who were at that time
in great distress and were lying on a completely broken
wreck, and on that same voyage he found Vinland the
Good. He arrived in Greenland late in the summer, and
went home to Brattahlid to his father Eric [the Red]. . . .

— 17 —

THE CREATION OF A BENEFICE, SEVENTH CENTURY [1]

The benefice bears a substantial relationship to the
precarium *found in Roman Law. Under the Merovingian*
kings, it was usually a grant of land to a church or mon-
astery by which the grantor held life use (usufruct) of
the property in return for some pious service by the
grantee. On the death of the grantor, the gift passed to
the church. Land was a chief source of wealth. In about
732 Charles Martel, looking for means to provide for a
cavalry force to repel Moslem raiders, compelled the
church to grant benefices to laymen in return for their
agreement to fight with him. Kings and powerful laymen
granted benefices to those who served them as a form of

[1] O. J. Thatcher and E. H. McNeal, *A Source Book for*
Mediaeval History (Charles Scribner's Sons, New York,
1905), pp. 345-346. Reprinted by permission of the publisher.

payment. After the collapse of the Carolingian empire, benefices held by individuals tended to become hereditary because the monarch was too weak to prevent this from happening. When this occurs, about the end of the ninth century, the benefice is called a fief.

. . . I, (name), and my wife, (name), in the name of the Lord, give by this letter of gift, and transfer from our ownership to the ownership and authority of the monastery of (name), over which the venerable abbot (name) presides, and which was founded in the honor of (name) by (name) in the county of (name), the following villas (name), situated in the county of (name), with all the lands, houses, buildings, tenants, slaves, vineyards, woods, fields, pastures, meadows, streams, and all other belongings and dependencies, and all things movable and immovable which are found in the said villas now or may be added later; in order that under the protection of Christ they may be used for the support and maintenance of the monks who dwell in the aforesaid monastery. We do this on the condition that as long as either of us shall live we may possess the aforesaid villas, without prejudice to the ownership of the monastery and without diminution of the value of them, except that we shall be allowed to emancipate any of the slaves that dwell on the lands for the salvation of our souls. After the death of both of us, the aforesaid villas with any additions or improvements which may have been made, shall return immediately to the possession of the said monastery and the said abbot and his successors, without undertaking any judicial process or obtaining the consent of the heirs.

— 18 —

THE GRANT OF AN IMMUNITY, SEVENTH CENTURY[1]

*As was the case with benefices, grants of immunity
were probably first received by the Church. It is evident
that they would be much sought after by laymen, because
they brought freedom from much royal interference.
Charlemagne was strong enough not to make such grants
and actually recovered power that had been previously
granted. But during the anarchy caused by the rebellions
of his grandsons and the invasions of the Northmen,
counts were able to obtain these charters once more. By
the end of the ninth century many could simply take the
privileges because of the ineffectual monarchy. The possession of power usually held by a king by individuals
is one of the characteristics of feudalism.*

↗   ↗   ↗

Therefore, may your greatness or perseverance know
that we have seen fit to concede by our ready will to *such
and such an* illustrious man, the vill named *so and so,*
situated in *such and such* a district, completely with its
whole proper boundary, as it has been possessed by *such
and such a one* or by our treasury, or is possessed at this
present time. Wherefore, by our present authority we
have decreed what we command shall be kept forever, that
the man aforesaid, *so and so,* should have conceded to
him *such and such* a vill as we have said, in its entirety,
with the lands, houses, buildings, villeins, slaves, vineyards, woods, fields, meadows, pastures, waters or water-
courses, grist mills, additions, appurtenances, or any kind
of men who are subjected to our treasury who dwell
there; in entire immunity, and without the entrance of any

[1] Univ. of Penn., "Trans. and Repr.," IV, 3, pp. 12-13.

one of the judges for the purpose of holding the pleas of
any kind of causes. Thus he may have, hold, and possess
it in proprietary right and without expecting the entrance
of any one of the judges; and may leave the possession
of it to his posterity, by the aid of God, from our bounty,
or to whom he will; and by our permission he shall have
free power to do whatever he may wish with it for the
future. And in order that this authority may be held as
more firm, we have decreed it to be corroborated below
with our own hand.

— 19 —

A FORMULA OF COMMENDATION, SEVENTH CENTURY [1]

*The Germans had a custom whereby lesser men would
voluntarily place themselves under the protection of
stronger men. The former would receive protection and
in return would perform certain duties for the latter. The
principle of commendation was well developed under the
Merovingian Franks.*

To that magnificent lord *so and so*, I, *so and so*. Since
it is know familiarly to all how little I have whence to
feed and clothe myself, I have therefore petitioned your
piety, and your good-will has decreed to me that I should
hand myself over or commend myself to your guardianship, which I have thereupon done; that is to say in this
way, that you should aid and succor me as well with
food as with clothing, according as I shall be able to serve
you and deserve it.

[1] Univ. of Penn., "Trans. and Rep.," IV, 3, pp. 3-4.

And so long as I shall live I ought to provide service and honor to you, suitably to my free condition; and I shall not during the time of my life have the ability to withdraw from your power or guardianship; but must remain during the days of my life under your power or defence. Wherefore it is proper that if either of us shall wish to withdraw himself from these agreements, he shall pay *so many* shillings to his peer and this agreement shall remain unbroken. . . .

— 20 —

THE CAPITULARY OF MERSEN, 847[1]

The development of personal dependency as shown in commendation becomes more common and formal in this document. The anarchy attendant on the disintegration of the Carolingian Empire, and the raids of the Northmen, Moslems, and Magyars greatly increased the need for physical protection. By the end of the ninth century, particularly in northern France and Germany, commendation had been imperceptibly altered to become the lord-vassal relationship of feudalism.

We will moreover that each free man in our kingdom shall choose a lord, from us or our faithful, such a one as he wishes.

We command moreover that no man shall leave his lord without just cause, nor should any one receive him, except in such a way as was customary in the time of our predecessors.

And we wish you to know that we want to grant right

[1] Univ. of Penn., "Trans. and Rep.," IV, 3, p. 5.

to our faithful subjects and we do not wish to do anything to them against reason. Similarly we admonish you and the rest of our faithful subjects that you grant right to your men and do not act against reason toward them.

And we will that the man of each one of us [Lothair, Louis and Charles] in whosesoever kingdom he is, shall go with his lord against the enemy, or in his other needs unless there shall have been (as may there not be) such an invasion of the kingdom as is called a *landwer,* so that the whole people of that kingdom shall go together to repel it.

— 21 —

THE CAPITULARY OF KIERSEY, 877[1]

Under Charlemagne the count was an official sent to govern a district for the emperor The ineffectual successors of Charlemagne lost control over the counts, who continued to exercise their authority for their own benefit, instead of as imperial representatives. By the end of the ninth century many counts had changed their titles to of instead of in such and such a place. A further step in the breakdown of central government and the development of feudalism was that the count's title, authority, and property should become hereditary. This capitulary of Charles the Bald (875-877), published just before he left France for a campaign in Italy, in effect endowed the comital nobility and recognized the independence it had obtained.

If a count of this kingdom, whose son is with us, shall die, our son with the rest of our faithful shall appoint

[1] Univ. of Penn., "Trans. and Rep.," IV, 3, p. 14.

some one of the nearest relatives of the same count, who, along with the officials of his province and with the bishop in whose diocese the same province is, shall administer that province until announcement is made to us, so that we may honor his son who is with us with his honors.

If, however, he had a minor son, this same son, along with the officials of that province and with the bishop in whose diocese it is, shall make provision for the same province until the notice of the death of the same count shall come to us, that his son may be honored, by our concession, with his honors.

If, however, he had no son, our son along with the rest of the faithful, shall take charge, who, along with the officials of the same province and with the proper bishop shall make provision for the same province until our order may be made in regard to it. Therefore, let him not be angry who shall provide for the province if we give the same province to another whom it pleases us, rather than to him who has so far provided for it.

Similarly also shall this be done concerning our vassals. And we will and command that as well the bishops as the abbots and the counts, and any others of our faithful also, shall study to preserve this toward their men.

— 22 —

EXTRACTS FROM "GLANVILLE" ON FEUDAL TENURE[1]

The treatise from which these selections are taken was composed about 1190, and the author is usually described

[1] David C. Douglas and George W. Greenaway, eds., *English Historical Documents* (13 vols., Eyre and Spottiswoode, London, 1953), II, 937-943, *passim*.

*as Ranulf de Glanville, justiciar of England from 1180
to 1189. Whether he or his nephew Hubert Walter, archbishop of Canterbury and justiciar under Richard I, or
an unknown person wrote the work, the author was most
familiar with the laws and customs of feudal England.*

✓   ✓   ✓

Book IX. *Chap. I.* It remains to continue upon the subject of performing homage and receiving reliefs. Upon the
death of the father or any other ancestor, the lord of the
fee is bound from the first to receive the homage of the
true heir, whether the heir has attained full age or not,
provided always that he be male. For females cannot by
law perform any homage, although, generally speaking,
they are wont to do fealty to their lords. But if they are
married their husbands ought to do homage to their lords
for their fee; if, I mean, homage be due in respect of such
fees. If, however, the heir be male and a minor, the lord
of the fee is not entitled by law to the wardship of the
heir or of his holding until he has received the homage
of the heir; because it is a general principle that no one
can exact from an heir, whether he is of age or not, any
service, whether a relief or otherwise, until he has received the homage of the heir in respect of that holding
for which the service is claimed. But a person may perform homage to several lords on account of different fees,
but of these homages one should be the chief and should
be liege homage, and this must be performed to the lord
from whom the person performing homage holds his chief
tenement. Homage ought to be done in this manner,
namely, that he who performs it shall so become the man
of his lord that he shall bear faith to him for the tenement in respect of which he performs homage, and shall
preserve the earthly honor of his lord in all things save
the faith due to the king and to his heirs. . . .

Chap. II. Homage is only due for lands, free tenements,
services, and dues, either of money or in kind, which have
been precisely determined. Only in respect of demesne
should homage be rendered to no one except to the king.
Yet homage ought not always to be performed for every
kind of land. Thus it is not due for land in dower or for
a marriage portion freely bestowed, nor from the fee of

younger sisters holding from the eldest, within the third descent on both sides; nor is it due from a fee given in frankalmoign, nor from any tenement given in any way as a marriage portion, so far as concerns the person of the husband of the woman to whom the property belongs as her marriage portion.

Chap. III. Homage may, however, be done to any free person whether male or female, whether of full age or otherwise, and whether clerk or lay. . . .

Chap. IV. There ought to be a reciprocal obligation of fidelity between lordship and homage. Nor does the tenant owe more to his lord in respect of homage than the lord owes to the tenant on account of lordship, reverence alone excepted. . . .

Chap. VIII. After it has been settled between the lord and the heir of the tenant concerning the giving and receiving of a reasonable relief, the heir may exact reasonable aids in respect of this from his own men. This, however, must be done with moderation in accordance with the number and resources of their fees lest they should be too much oppressed or should lose their contenement.[1] But nothing certain is fixed concerning the giving and exacting of aids of this kind except that the conditions we have noted must be always observed. There are also other cases in which a lord can exact from his men similar aids, always observing the prescribed form: as when his son and heir is made a knight, and when he gives his eldest daughter in marriage. But whether lords can exact aids to maintain private war is doubtful. The opinion which prevails is that they cannot lawfully distrain their tenants for such a purpose except in so far as the tenants agree. But with respect to the payment of reasonable aids, lords may of their own right, without the king's precept or that of his justices, but by the judgment of their own court, distrain their tenants by such of their chattels as may be found within their fees or if necessary by their fees themselves; provided always that the tenants are dealt with according to the judgment of the lord's court and consistently with its reasonable custom. If therefore a lord may thus distrain his tenants to

[1] *Contenementum* is the property necessary to enable a man to maintain his position.

pay such reasonable aids, much stronger is the argument that he may lawfully distrain in the same manner for a relief, or for any other service necessarily due to him in respect of the fee. . . .

— 23 —

CHARTER OF HOMAGE AND FEALTY OF THE VISCOUNT OF CARCASSONNE, 1110[1]

This document illustrates the mutual obligations of lord and vassal in feudalism. It may also emphasize the fact that ecclesiastics also were feudal lords. No two contracts were exactly alike; they differed in details, and customs varied in the various regions of Europe where feudalism existed. Attention may be drawn to the third paragraph, which stipulates exactly what Bernard Atton must provide, for lords often tried to increase the purveyance due them.

✓   ✓   ✓

In the name of the Lord, I, Bernard Atton, Viscount of Carcassonne, in the presence of my sons, Roger and Trencavel, and of Peter Roger of Barbazan, and William Hugo, and Raymond Mantellini, and Peter de Vietry, nobles, and of many other honorable men, who had come to the monastery of St. Mary of Grasse, to the honor of the festival of the august St. Mary; since lord Leo, abbot of the said monastery, has asked me, in the presence of all those above mentioned, to acknowledge to him the fealty and homage for the castles, manors, and places

[1] Univ. of Penn., "Trans. and Rep.," IV, 3, pp. 18-20.

which the patrons, my ancestors, held from him and his predecessors and from the said monastery as a fief, and which I ought to hold as they held, I have made to the lord abbot Leo acknowledgment and homage as I ought to do.

Therefore, let all present and to come know that I the said Bernard Atton, lord and viscount of Carcassonne, acknowledge verily to thee my lord Leo, by the grace of God, abbot of St. Mary of Grasse, and to thy successors that I hold and ought to hold as a fief, in Carcassonne, the following: . . . Moreover, I acknowledge that I hold from thee and from the said monastery as a fief the castle of Termes in Narbonne; and in Minerve the castle of Ventaion, and the manors of Cassanolles, and of Ferral and Aiohars; and in Le Rogès, the little village of Long-ville; for each and all of which I make homage and fealty with hands and with mouth to thee my said lord abbot Leo and to thy successors, and I swear upon these four gospels of God that I will always be a faithful vassal to thee and to thy successors and to St. Mary of Grasse in all things in which a vassal is required to be faithful to his lord, and I will defend thee, my lord, and all thy successors, and the said monastery and the monks present and to come and the castles and manors and all your men and their possessions against all malefactors and invaders, at my request and that of my successors at my own cost; and I will give to thee power over all the castles and manors above described, in peace and in war, whenever they shall be claimed by thee or by thy successors.

Moreover I acknowledge that, as a recognition of the above fiefs, I and my successors ought to come to the said monastery, at our own expense, as often as a new abbot shall have been made, and there do homage and return to him the power over all the fiefs described above. And when the abbot shall mount his horse I and my heirs, viscounts of Carcassonne, and our successors ought to hold the stirrup for the honor of the dominion of St. Mary of Grasse; and to him and all who come with him, to as many as two hundred beasts, we should make the abbot's purveyance in the borough of St. Michael of Carcassonne, the first time he enters Carcassonne, with the best fish and meat and with eggs and cheese, honorably according to his will, and pay the expense of the shoeing of the horses, and for straw and fodder as the season shall require.

And if I or my sons or their successors do not observe to thee or to thy successors each and all the things declared above, and should come against these things, we wish that all the aforesaid fiefs should by that very fact be handed over to thee and to the said monastery of St. Mary of Grasse and to thy successors.

I, therefore, the aforesaid lord Leo, by the grace of God, abbot of St. Mary of Grasse, receive thy homage and fealty for all the fiefs of castles and manors and places which are described above; in the way and with the agreements and understandings written above; and likewise I concede to thee and thy heirs and their successors, the viscounts of Carcassonne, all the castles and manors and places aforesaid, as a fief, along with this present charter, divided through the alphabet. And I promise to thee and thy heirs and successors, viscounts of Carcassonne, under the religion of my order, that I will be good and faithful lord concerning all those things described above.

Moreover, I, the aforesaid viscount, acknowledge that the little villages of [twelve are listed] with the farmhouse of Mathus and the chateaux of Villalauro and Claromont, with the little villages of St. Stephen of Surlac, and of Upper and Lower Agrifolio, ought to belong to the said monastery, and whoever holds anything there holds from the same monastery, as we have seen and have heard read in the privileges and charters of the monastery, and as was there written.

Made in the year of the Incarnation of the Lord 1110, in the reign of Louis. Seal of [the witnesses named in paragraph one, Bernard Atton and abbot Leo] who has accepted this acknowledgment of the homage of the said viscount.

And I, the monk John, have written this charter at the command of the said lord Bernard Atton, viscount of Carcassonne and of his sons, on the day and year given above, in the presence and witness of all those named above.

— 24 —

THE OBLIGATIONS OF A DEPENDENCY OF THE PAPACY, ca. 1116[1]

The papacy held vast amounts of land throughout Europe from which it received income and services. It needed and developed an elaborate organization to collect its due, while at Rome there was an efficient department in the papal curia concerned with these affairs. The town of Nimfa mentioned in this document is an ancient village in east central Italy and was given to the papacy by the Byzantine emperor Constantine VIII (963-1028).

✦   ✦   ✦

These are the things which the people of Nimfa should do. They should do fealty to St. Peter and Lord Pope Paschal and his successors whom the higher cardinals and the Romans may elect. Service of army and court when the court may command. The service which they have been accustomed to do, and plea and ban, they should do to St. Peter and the pope. The fourth which they ought to render henceforth, they should render at the measure of the Roman modius; and if the bailiff orders, they should carry it to Tiber or Cisterna. They should pay pannage on the festival of St. Martin; good hind quarters of meat on the festival of St. Thomas. For each load of grain they should pay six pence. Tribute in each year, in the month of May, thirty good pounds of Pavia. The toll which they ought to pay outside should be paid to the court. The procuration which they had

[1] William E. Lunt, *Papal Revenues in the Middle Ages* (Records of Civilization, XIX, Columbia University Press, New York, 1934), II, pp. 11-12.

owed to the lord pope for one day they should give for
two. The mills which the lord pope now holds, namely,
twelve which are outside and one which is above the
reservoir, they should release acquitted. The wall of the
city they should destroy according to the command of the
court, nor should they build it without its license.

— 25 —

SERVICES DUE FROM
A VILLEIN, 1307[1]

*John of Cayworth held his land from Battle Abbey and
it was part of the manor of Bernehorn in Sussex, England. The manor consisted of over 682 acres, of which
489 acres were in the demesne and the remaining 193
were divided among eight free tenants, seven villeins, and
eighteen cotters. The services and status of John of Cayworth were about those of the typical serf. It will be noticed that some of the services produced a loss for the
lord; as these instances increased, the landlord tended to
free his serfs. They would then be available for work at
daily wages, which would cost him less than servile labor.*

✔   ✔   ✔

They say that John of Cayworth holds one house and
thirty acres of land, and he owes 2 *s.* a year at Easter and
Michaelmas, and he owes one cock and two hens at
Christmas worth 4 *s.*

And he ought to harrow for two days at the sowing at
Lent with one man and his own horse and harrow, the
value of the work is 4 *d.*; and he receives from the lord

[1] S. R. Scargill-Bird, ed., *Custumals of Battle Abbey* (The
Camden Society, 1887), pp. 19-23.

on each day three meals worth 3 *d.*; and the lord will thus lose 1 *d.*; and so this harrowing is worth nothing to the service of the lord.

And he ought to carry the manure of the lord for two days with one cart using his own two oxen, the work to value 8 *s.*, and he receives from the lord three meals of the above value each day; and so the work is worth 3 *d.* clear.

And he should find one man for two days to mow the meadow of the lord, who can mow an estimated one acre and a half: the value of mowing one acre is 6 *d.*; and the total is 9 *d.*; and he receives for each day three meals of the above value, and thus the mowing is worth 4 *d.* clear.

And he ought to collect and carry that same hay which he has mowed, the value of the work is 3 *d.* And he has from the lord two meals for one man worth 1½ *d.*; thus the work is worth 1½ *d.* clear.

And he ought to carry the hay of the lord for one day with one cart and three animals of his own, the price of the work is 6 *d.*; and he has from the lord three meals worth 2½ *d.*; and thus the work has a value of 3½ *d.* clear.

And he ought to carry in the autumn beans or oats for two days with one cart and three of his own animals, the price of the work is 12 *d.*; and he has from the lord three meals of the above price for each day, and thus the work is worth 7 *d.* clear.

And he ought to carry wood from the woods of the lord to the manor house for two days in summer with one cart and three of his own animals, the price of the work is 9 *d.*; and he receives from the lord for each day three meals of the above price. And so the work is worth 4 *d.* clear.

And he ought to find one man for two days to cut heath, the price of the work is 4 [*d.*]; and he will have three meals for each day of the above price; and so the lord loses if he receives the work 1 *d.*; and thus that cutting is worth nothing to the work of the lord.

And he ought to carry the heath that he has cut, the price of the work is 5 *d.*; and he receives from the lord three meals of the price of 2½ *d.*; and thus the work is worth 2½ *d.* clear.

And he ought to carry to Battle [Abbey] two times in the summer half a load of grain each time, the price of the work is 4 *d.*; and he will receive in the manor each time one meal worth 2 *d.*; and thus the work is worth 2 *d.* clear.

The sum of the rents, with the price of the chickens is 2 *s.* 4 *d.*; the sum of the value of the work is 2 *s.* 3½ *d.*; owed from the said John per year. . . .

And it must be noted that all the aforesaid villeins may not marry their daughters nor have their sons tonsured, nor can they cut down timber growing on the lands they hold, without the personal approval of the bailiff or servant of the lord, and then for building and no other purpose.

And after the death of any one of the aforesaid villeins the lord will have as a heriot the best animal that he had; if, however, he had no living beast, the lord will have no heriot, as they say.

The sons or daughters of the aforesaid villeins will give to enter the tenement after the death of their ancestors as much as they gave in rent per year.

— 26 —

DICTATUS PAPAE, 1075 [1]

There is some debate as to whether or not Pope Gregory VII wrote these sentences that reflect his ideas. They were composed early in 1075 and represent the extreme claims of the Papacy. Henry IV and the imperial

[1] E. F. Henderson, *Historical Documents of the Middle Ages* (George Bell & Sons, London, 1896), pp. 366-367. Cited hereafter as Henderson, *Documents.*

party rejected most of them, and not all were acceptable to many of the higher clergy.

ⵏ   ⵏ   ⵏ

That the Roman church was founded by God alone.

That the Roman pontiff alone can with right be called universal.

That he alone can depose or reinstate bishops.

That, in a council, his legate, even if a lower grade, is above all bishops, and can pass sentence of deposition against them.

That the pope may depose the absent.

That, among other things, we ought not to remain in the same house with those excommunicated by him.

That for him alone is it lawful, according to the needs of the time, to make new laws, to assemble together new congregations, to make an abbey of a canonry; and, on the other hand, to divide a rich bishopric and unite the poor ones.

That he alone may use the imperial insignia.

That of the pope alone all princes shall kiss the feet.

That his name alone shall be spoken in the churches.

That this is the only name in the world.

That it may be permitted to him to depose emperors.

That he may be permitted to transfer bishops if need be.

That he has power to ordain a clerk of any church he may wish.

That he who is ordained by him may *preside* over another church, but may not hold a subordinate position; and that such a one may not receive a higher grade from any bishop.

That no synod shall be called a general one without his order.

That no chapter and no book shall be considered canonical without his authority.

That a sentence passed by him may be retracted by no one; and that he himself, alone of all, may retract it.

That he himself may be judged by no one.

That no one shall dare to condemn one who appeals to the apostolic chair.

That to the latter should be referred the more important cases of every church.

That the Roman church has never erred; nor will it err to all eternity, the Scriptures bearing witness.

That the Roman pontiff, if he have been canonically ordained, is undoubtedly made a saint by the merits of St. Peter; St. Ennodius, bishop of Pavia, bearing witness, and many holy fathers agreeing with him. As is contained in the decrees of St. Symmachus the pope.

That, by his command and consent, it may be lawful for subordinates to bring accusations.

That he may depose and reinstate bishops without assembling a synod.

That he who is not at peace with the Roman church shall not be considered catholic.

That he may absolve subjects from their fealty to wicked men.

— 27 —

LETTER OF HENRY IV TO GREGORY VII, 1076 [1]

This letter is presumably in answer to one from the Pope in which Gregory warned Henry not to associate with those who had been excommunicated and to obtain absolution. He also chastised Henry for appointing bishops to Italian sees, and indicated a willingness to discuss the points of difference between them. But the pope cautiously withheld his judgment of Henry until his legates discussed various matters with him and returned to report to Gregory. This letter is a moved statement of Henry's views. When put opposite the Dictatus Papae, the gulf that separated the two men is evident.

[1] Henderson, *Documents*, pp. 372-373.

Henry, king not through usurpation but through the holy ordination of God, to Hildebrand, at present not pope but false monk. Such greeting as this hast thou merited through thy disturbances, inasmuch as there is no grade in the church which thou hast omitted to make a partaker not of honor but of confusion, not of benediction but of malediction. For, to mention few and especial cases out of many, not only hast thou not feared to lay hands upon the rulers of the holy church, the anointed of the Lord—the archbishops, namely, bishops and priests —but thou hast trodden them under foot like slaves ignorant of what their master is doing. Thou hast won favor from the common herd by crushing them; thou hast looked upon all of them as knowing nothing, upon thy sole self, moreover, as knowing all things. This knowledge, however, thou hast used not for edification but for destruction; so that with reason we believe that St. Gregory, whose name thou hast usurped for thyself, was prophesying concerning thee when he said: "The pride of him who is in power increases the more, the greater the number of those subject to him; and he thinks that he himself can do more than all." And we, indeed, have endured all this, being eager to guard the honor of the apostolic see; thou, however, hast understood our humility to be fear, and hast not, accordingly, shunned to rise up against the royal power conferred upon us by God, daring to threaten to divest us of it. As if we had received our kingdom from thee! As if the kingdom and the empire were in thine and not in God's hands! And this although our Lord Jesus Christ did call us to the kingdom, did not, however, call thee to the priesthood. For thou hast ascended by the following steps. By wiles, namely, which the profession of monk abhors, thou hast achieved money; by money, favor; by the sword, the throne of peace. And from the throne of peace thou hast disturbed peace, inasmuch as thou hast armed subjects against those in authority over them; inasmuch as thou, who wert not called, hast taught that our bishops called of God are to be despised; inasmuch as thou hast usurped for laymen the ministry over their priests, allowing them to depose or condemn those whom they themselves had received as teachers from the hand of God through the laying on of hands of the bishops. On me also who, although unworthy to be among the anointed, have nevertheless been anointed to the kingdom, thou hast lain thy hand; me who —as the tradition of the holy Fathers teaches, declaring that I am not to be deposed for any crime unless, which God forbid, I should have strayed from the faith—am subject to the judgment of God alone. For the wisdom of the holy fathers committed even Julian the apostate not to themselves, but to God alone, to be judged and to be deposed. For himself the true pope, Peter, also exclaims: "Fear God, honor the king." But thou dost not fear God, dost dishonor in me his appointed one. Wherefore St. Paul, when he has not spared an angel of Heaven if he shall have preached otherwise, has not expected thee also who dost teach otherwise upon earth. For he says: "If any one, either I or an angel from Heaven, should preach a gospel other than that which has been preached to you, he shall be damned. Thou, therefore, damned by this curse and by the judgment of all our bishops and by our own, descend and relinquish the apostolic chair which thou hast usurped. Let another ascend the throne of St. Peter, who shall not practice violence under the cloak of religion, but shall teach the sound doctrine of St. Peter. I Henry, king by the grace of God, do say unto thee, together with all our bishops: Descend, descend, to be damned throughout the ages.

— 28 —

THE FIRST EXCOMMUNICATION AND DEPOSITION OF HENRY IV, FEBRUARY, 1076[1]

Henry IV was excommunicated and deposed by a council summoned to Rome by Gregory VII in February 1076. With this act Gregory established a precedent, and the German princes quickly organized a revolt against their rigorous monarch. The Saxons once more revolted as did the powerful dukes of Carinthia, Bavaria, and Swabia. Henry was beaten and knew it. The nobles demanded that Henry surrender, and he did in October; but it is interesting that the German clergy in general were more loyal to Henry. Gregory addressed a letter to them in the spring explaining his attitude, but it did not move them. Note that this document is addressed to St. Peter.

✦   ✦   ✦

O St. Peter, chief of the apostles, incline to us, I beg, thy holy ears, and hear my thy servant whom thou hast nourished from infancy, and whom, until this day, thou hast freed from the hand of the wicked, who have hated and do hate me for my faithfulness to thee. Thou, and my mistress the mother of God, and thy brother St. Paul are witnesses for me among all the saints that thy holy Roman church drew me to its helm against my will; that I had no thought of ascending thy chair through force, and that I would rather have ended my life as a pilgrim than, by secular means, to have seized thy throne for the sake of earthly glory. And therefore I believe it to be through thy grace and not through my own deeds that it has pleased and does please thee that the Christian people,

[1] Henderson, *Documents,* pp. 376-377.

who have been especially committed to thee, should obey me. And especially to me, as thy representative and by thy favor, has the power been granted by God of binding and loosing in Heaven and on earth. On the strength of this belief therefore, for the honor and security of thy church, in the name of Almighty God, Father, Son and Holy Ghost, I withdraw, through thy power and authority, from Henry the king, son of Henry the emperor, who has risen against thy church with unheard of insolence, the rule over the whole kingdom of the Germans and over Italy. And I absolve all Christians from the bonds of the oath which they have made or shall make to him; and I forbid any one to serve him as king. For it is fitting that he who strives to lessen the honor of thy church should himself lose the honor which belongs to him. And since he has scorned to obey as a Christian, and has not returned to God whom he had deserted—holding intercourse with the excommunicated; practising manifold iniquities; spurning my commands which, as thou dost bear witness, I issued to him for his own salvation; separating himself from thy church and striving to rend it—I bind him in thy stead with the chain of the anathema. And, leaning on thee, I so bind him that the people may know and have proof that thou art Peter, and above thy rock the Son of the living God hath built His church, and the gates of Hell shall not prevail against it.

— 29 —

GREGORY VII DESCRIBES THE PENANCE OF HENRY IV AT CANOSSA, 1077[1]

Henry realized that his only hope was to reach the pope before he arrived in Germany whither he had been invited by the princes. Gregory VII had come to the castle at Canossa of Countess Mathilda of Tuscany, and there awaited a safe-conduct to enter Germany. In the meanwhile, however, Henry and a small group were making their way by a circuitous route, the main roads being watched by the rebellious nobles, over the Mt. Cenis pass and literally sliding down its icy slopes into Italy. He presented himself as a penitent before the castle in January. Within its walls, besides the hostess and her guest, was Henry's godfather, the abbot of Cluny and a number of high ecclesiastics.

✓   ✓   ✓

. . . He [Henry] also, before entering Italy, sent on to us suppliant legates, offering in all things to render satisfaction to God, to St. Peter and to us. And he renewed his promise that, besides amending his life, he would observe all obedience if only he might merit to obtain from us the favor of absolution and the apostolic benediction. When, after long deferring this and holding frequent consultations, we had, through all the envoys who passed, severely taken him to task for his excesses: he came at length of his own accord, with a few followers, showing nothing of hostility or boldness, to the town of Canossa where we were tarrying. And there, having laid aside all the belongings of royalty, wretchedly, with bare feet and

[1] Henderson, *Documents*, pp. 386-387.

clad in wool, he continued for three days to stand before the gate of the castle. Nor did he desist from imploring with many tears the aid and consolation of the apostolic mercy until he had moved all of those who were present there, and whom the report of it reached, to such pity and depth of compassion that, interceding for him with many prayers and tears, all wondered indeed at the unaccustomed hardness of our heart, while some actually cried out that we were exercising, not the gravity of apostolic severity, but the cruelty, as it were, of a tyrannical ferocity.

Finally, conquered by the persistency of his compunction and by the constant supplications of all those who were present, we loosed the chain of the anathema and at length received him into the favor of communion and into the lap of the holy mother church. . . .

— 30 —

THE SECOND EXCOMMUNICATION AND DEPOSITION OF HENRY IV, 1080[1]

By coming to Canossa Henry had regained the church, but he had lost his point. The pope could judge monarchs. The rebellious Germans were dissatisfied, and in March elected an anti-king, Rudolf, duke of Swabia. Three years later, however, Henry had strengthened himself to the point where he asked Gregory to depose Rudolf; instead Gregory deposed Henry a second time. The result was to be that Henry marched into Italy. In 1083 he cap-

[1] Henderson, *Documents*, pp. 388-391.

*tured Rome. The Normans recaptured the city the next
year, and after subjecting it to a brutal sack, withdrew,
taking the hapless Gregory with them. He died, asserting
his claims to the end, in May 1085.*

✓   ✓   ✓

St. Peter, chief of the apostles, and thou St. Paul,
teacher of the nations, deign, I beg, to incline your ears
to me and mercifully to hear me. Do ye who are the
disciples and lovers of truth aid me to tell the truth to ye
without any of the falsehood which we altogether detest:
to the end that my brothers may better acquiesce with me
and may know and learn that, after God and his mother
the ever-Virgin Mary, it is in ye I trust when I resist the
wicked and unholy but lend aid to your faithful followers.
For ye know that I did not willingly take holy orders.
And unwillingly I went with my master Gregory beyond
the mountains; but more unwillingly I returned with my
master pope Leo to your especial church, in which I
served ye as always. Then, greatly against my will, with
much grieving and groaning and wailing I was placed
upon your throne, although thoroughly unworthy. I say
these things thus because I did not choose ye but ye chose
me and did place upon me the very heavy burden of your
church. And because ye did order me to go up into a high
mountain and call out and proclaim to the people of God
their crimes and to the sons of the earth their sins, the
members of the devil have commenced to rise up against
me and have presumed, even unto blood, to lay their
hands upon me. For the kings of the earth stood by, and
the secular and ecclesiastical princes; the men of the
palace, also, and the common herd came together against
the Lord and against ye His annointed, saying: "Let us
break their chains and cast off their yoke from us." And
they have in many ways attempted to rise up against me
in order to utterly confound me with death or with exile.

Among them, especially, Henry whom they call king,
son of Henry the emperor, did raise his heel against your
church and strive, by casting me down, to subjugate it,
having made a conspiracy with many ultramontane bishops. But your authority resisted and your power destroyed
their pride. He, confounded and humbled, came to me in

Lombardy and sought absolution from the bann. I, seeing him humiliated, having received many promises from him concerning the bettering of his way of living, restored to him the communion. But only that; I did not reinstate him in his kingdom from which I had deposed him in a Roman synod, nor did I order that the fealty from which, in that synod, I had absolved all those who had sworn it to him, or were about to swear it, should be observed towards him. And my reason for not doing so was that I might do justice in the matter or arrange peace—as Henry himself, by an oath before two bishops, had promised me should be done—between him and the ultramontane bishops or princes who, being commanded to do so by your church, had resisted him. But the said ultramontane bishops and princes, hearing that he had not kept his promise to me, and, as it were, despairing of him, elected for themselves without my advice—ye are my witness—duke Rudolf as king. This king Rudolf hastily sent an envoy to intimate to me that he had been compelled to accept the helm of state but that he was ready to obey me in every way. And to make this the more credible he has continued from that time to send me words to the same effect, adding also that he was ready to confirm what he had promised by giving his own son and the son of his faithful follower duke Bertald as hostages. Meanwhile Henry commenced to implore my aid against the said Rudolf. I answered that I would willingly grant it if I could hear the arguments on both sides so as to know whom justice most favored. But he, thinking to conquer by his own strength, scorned my reply. But when he found that he could not do as he had hoped he sent to Rome two of his partisans, the bishops, namely, of Verdun and of Osnabrück, who asked me in a synod to do justice to him. This also the envoys of Rudolf pressed me to do. At length, by God's inspiration as I believe, I decreed in that synod that an assembly should take place beyond the mountains, where either peace should be established or it should be made known which side justice the most favored. For I—as ye, my fathers and masters, can testify—have taken care up to this time to aid no party save the one on whose side justice should be found to be. And, thinking that the weaker side would wish the assembly not to take place, whereas justice would hold its own, I excommunicated and bound with the anathema the person of anyone—whether king, duke, bishop or ordinary man —who should by any means contrive to prevent the assembly from taking place. But the said Henry with his partisans, not fearing the danger from disobedience, which is the crime of idolatry, incurred the excommunication by impeding the assembly. And he bound himself with the chain of the anathema, causing a great multitude of Christians to be given over to death and of churches to be ruined, and rendering desolate almost the whole realm of the Germans. Wherefore, trusting in the judgment and mercy of God and of his most holy mother the ever-virgin Mary, armed with your authority, I lay under excommunication and bind with the chains of the anathema the oft-mentioned Henry—the so-called king—and all his followers. And again, on the part of God Almighty and of yourselves, I deny to him the kingdom of the Germans and of Italy and I take away from him all royal power and dignity. And I forbid any Christian to obey him as king, and absolve from their oath all who have sworn or shall swear to him as ruler of the land. May this same Henry, moreover—as well as his partisans—be powerless in any warlike encounter and obtain no victory during his life. Whereas I grant and concede in your name that Rudolf, whom, as a mark of fidelity to ye, the Germans have chosen to be their king, may rule and defend the land of the Germans. To all those who faithfully adhere to him I, trusting in your support, grant absolution of all their sins and your benediction in this life and the life to come. For as Henry, on account of his pride, disobedience and falseness, is justly cast down from his royal dignity, so to Rudolf, for his humility, obedience and truthfulness, the power and dignity of kingship are granted.

Proceed now, I beg, O fathers and most holy princes, in such way that all the world may learn and know that, if ye can bind and loose in Heaven, so ye can on earth take away empires, kingdoms, principalities, duchies, margravates, counties and all possessions of men, and grant them to any man ye please according to his merits. For often have ye taken away patriarchates, primateships, archbishoprics and bishoprics from the wicked and unworthy and given them to devout men. And if ye judge spiritual offices what are we to believe of your power in secular ones? And if ye shall judge angels, who rule over all proud princes, how will it be with those subject to them? Let kings and all secular princes now learn how great ye are and what your power is; and let them dread to disregard the command of your church. And, in the case of the said Henry, exercise such swift judgment that all may know him to fall not by chance but by your power. Let him be confounded;—would it were to repentance, that his soul may be safe at the day of the Lord!

Given at Rome, on the Nones of March, in the third indiction.

— 31 —

THE CONCORDAT OF WORMS, 1122[1]

This, at last, is the settlement of the investiture quarrel between the emperors and popes. Both sides gave in a little, but it would seem that in Germany the emperor had managed to keep the upper hand.

ィ　　　　　ィ　　　　　ィ

PRIVILEGE OF POPE CALIXTUS II

I, bishop Calixtus, servant of the servants of God, do grant to thee beloved son, Henry—by the grace of God august emperor of the Romans—that the elections of the bishops and abbots of the German kingdom, who belong to the kingdom, shall take place in thy presence, without

[1] Henderson, *Documents*, pp. 408-409.

simony and without any violence; so that if any discord shall arise between the parties concerned, thou, by the counsel or judgment of the metropolitan and the co-provincials, may'st give consent and aid to the party which has the more right. The one elected, moreover, without any exaction may receive the regalia from thee through the lance, and shall do unto thee for these what he rightfully should. But he who is consecrated in the other parts of the empire [*i.e.* Burgundy and Italy] shall, within six months, and without any exaction, receive the regalia from thee through the lance, and shall do unto thee for these what he rightfully should. Excepting all things which are known to belong to the Roman church. Concerning matters, however, in which thou dost make complaint to me, and dost demand aid,—I, according to the duty of my office, will furnish aid to thee. I give unto thee true peace, and to all who are or have been on thy side in the time of this discord.

EDICT OF EMPEROR HENRY V

In the name of the holy and indivisible Trinity, I, Henry, by the grace of God august emperor of the Romans, for the love of God and of the holy Roman church and of our master pope Calixtus, and for the healing of my soul, do remit to God, and to the holy apostles of God, Peter and Paul, and to the holy catholic church, all investiture through ring and staff; and do grant that in all the churches that are in my kingdom or empire there may be canonical election and free consecration. All the possessions and regalia of St. Peter which, from the beginning of this discord unto this day, whether in the time of my father or also in mine, have been abstracted, and which I hold: I restore to that same holy Roman church. As to those things, moreover, which I do not hold, I will faithfully aid in their restoration. As to the possessions also of all other churches and princes, and of all other lay and clerical persons which have been lost in that war: according to the counsel of the princes, or according to justice, I will restore the things that I hold; and of those things which I do not hold I will faithfully aid in the restoration. And I grant true peace to our master pope Calixtus, and to the holy Roman church, and to all those who are or have been on its side. And in matters where the holy Roman church shall demand aid I will grant it; and in matters concerning which it shall make complaint to me I will duly grant to it justice. All these things have been done by the consent and counsel of the princes. Whose names are here adjoined: [the names follow].

— 32 —

THE LAWS OF WILLIAM THE CONQUEROR[1]

There are two principal sources for the laws of William the Conqueror. The first and largest body consists of the laws of his predecessors that he confirmed. The second is contained in the document below and is his actual enactment. The manuscript from which they are taken was written in the reign of his son, Henry I, and seems to be a compilation of some ten laws. The sixth paragraph contains the first mention of trial by battle, which the Normans introduced to England.

Here is shown that William, king of the English, together with his princes, established after the Conquest of England.

1. Firstly, above everything, he wishes one God to be worshipped throughout all his kingdom, one faith in Christ always to be kept inviolate, peace and tranquility to be preserved between the English and Normans.

[1] William Stubbs, *Select Charters* (Oxford, 1884), pp. 83-85.
Cited hereafter as Stubbs, *Charters*.

2. We ordain furthermore that every free man shall assert by a covenant and an oath that, within and without England, they wish to be loyal to king William, to protect with him his lands and his honor with all faithfulness, and to defend him against his enemies.

3. I will, moreover, that all the men whom I have brought with me, or who have come after me, may live in my peace and quiet. And if one of them is killed, his murderer's lord shall capture the slayer within five days if he can; but if not, he shall start to pay to me forty-six marks of silver so long as his possessions last. But when they are exhausted, the whole hundred in which the slaying occurred shall pay in common what remains.

4. And every Frenchman who, in the time of my relative king Edward, partook in England of the customs of the English, shall pay according to the law of the English what they call "scot and lot." This decree was confirmed in the city of Gloucester.

5. We forbid also that any live cattle be sold or bought for money except within the cities, and before three faithful witnesses; nor even anything old without a surety and warrant. But if anyone does otherwise he shall pay and afterwards pay a fine.

6. It was also decreed there that if a Frenchman accuses an Englishman of perjury or murder, theft, homicide, "ran," as the English call open pillaging which can not be denied, the Englishman may defend himself as he prefers, either through the ordeal of hot water or through trial by battle. But if the Englishman is infirm, he shall find someone else who will do it for him. If one of them shall be defeated he shall pay a fine of forty shillings to the king. If an Englishman accuses a Frenchman, and is unwilling to prove his charge by ordeal or trial by battle, I will, nevertheless, that the Frenchman purge himself by a strong oath.

7. This also I command and will, that all shall have and keep the law of king Edward with regard to their lands and all their possessions, together with those additions which I have established for the benefit of the English people.

8. Every man who wishes to be considered a freeman shall have a surety, in order that his surety may hold him

and hand him over to justice if he gives offence in any way. And if any such one escape, his surcties shall directly see to it that they pay what is charged against him, and clear themselves of knowledge of any deceit in his escape. The hundred and county court shall be required as our predecessors decreed. And those who ought of right to come, and are unwilling to come, shall be summoned once; and if a second time they do not wish to come, one ox shall be taken from them and they shall be summoned a third time. And if they do not come the third time, another ox shall be taken. Moreover, if they do not come the fourth time there shall be handed over from the goods of that man who was unwilling to come, the amount of the charge against him, which is called "ceapgeld"; and additionally a fine to the king.

9. I prohibit any man to sell another outside the country under penalty of a fine paid in full to me.

10. I also forbid that any one be killed or hung for any crime, but his eyes shall be torn out and his testicles cut off. And this command shall not be violated under penalty of a fine paid in full to me.

— 33 —

THE SPEECH OF POPE URBAN II AT CLERMONT, NOVEMBER 26, 1095 [1]

There are four versions of this speech by persons who were probably present, but who do not pretend to quote Urban's words exactly. He had been asked for help by the

[1] Univ. of Penn., "Trans. and Rep.," I, 2, pp. 2-5.

Emperor Alexius against the Saljuq Turks, and after presiding at the Council of Piacenza in the spring of 1095, he had come to France. In the course of the summer he stayed at Toulouse, Cluny, and other places where he dedicated new cathedrals, churches, and altars. While there is disagreement as to why Urban preached the crusade, it is probable that he had worked out the idea in discussions with lay and clerical nobles and that his speech was not unprepared. This version is by Fulcher of Chartres.

ʎ   ʎ   ʎ

Most beloved brethren, moved by the exigencies of the times, I, Urban, wearing by the permission of God the papal tiara, and spiritual ruler of the whole world, have come here to you, the servants of God, as a messenger to disclose the divine admonition. I desire that those whom I have believed to be the faithful servants of God shall show themselves such, and that there shall be no shameful dissimulation. But if there is in you, contrary to God's law, any deformity or crookedness, because you have lost the moderation of reason and justice, I will earnestly strive to root out the fault. . . .

Since, oh sons of God, you have promised the Lord more earnestly than heretofore to maintain peace in your midst and faithfully to sustain the laws of the church, there remains for you, newly fortified by the correction of the Lord, to show the strength of your integrity in a certain other duty, which is not less your concern than the Lord's. For you must carry succor to your brethren dwelling in the East, and needing your aid, which they have so often demanded. . . .

Wherefore, I pray and exhort, nay not I, but the Lord prays and exhorts you, as heralds of Christ, by frequent exhortation, to urge men of all ranks, knights and foot-soldiers, rich and poor, to hasten to exterminate this vile race from the lands of our brethren, and to bear timely aid to the worshippers of Christ. I speak to those who are present, I proclaim it to the absent, but Christ commands. Moreover, the sins of those who set out thither, if they lose their lives on the journey, by land or sea, or in fighting against the heathen, shall be remitted in that hour;

this I grant to all who go, through the power of God vested in me.

Oh, what a disgrace if a race so despised, degenerate, and slave of the demons, should thus conquer a people fortified with faith in omnipotent God and resplendent with the name of Christ! Oh, how many reproaches will be heaped upon you by the Lord Himself if you do not aid those who like yourselves are counted of the Christian faith! Let those who have formerly been accustomed to contend wickedly in private warfare against the faithful, fight against the infidel and bring to a victorious end the war which ought long since to have begun. Let those who have hitherto been robbers now become soldiers of Christ. Let those who have formerly contended against their brothers and relatives now fight as they ought against the barbarians. Let those who have formerly been mercenaries at low wages, now gain eternal rewards. Let those who have been striving to the detriment both of body and soul, now labor for a two-fold reward. . . .

Extracts from the version by Robert the Monk[2]

From the confines of Jerusalem and the city of Constantinople a horrible tale has gone forth and very frequently has been brought to our ears, namely, that a race from the kingdom of the Persians, an accursed race, a race utterly alienated from God, a generation forsooth which has not directed its heart and has not entrusted its spirit to God, has invaded the lands of those Christians and has depopulated them by the sword, pillage and fire; it has led away a part of the captives into its own country, and a part it has destroyed by cruel tortures; it has either entirely destroyed the churches of God or appropriated them for the rites of its own religion. They destroy the altars, after having defiled them with their uncleanness. They circumcise the Christians, and the blood of the circumcision they either spread upon the altars or pour into the vases of the baptismal font. When they wish to torture people by a base death, they perforate their navels, and dragging forth the extremity of the intestines, bind it to a stake; then with flogging they lead the victim around

[2] *Ibid.,* pp. 5-8.

until the viscera having gushed forth the victim falls prostrate upon the ground. Others they bind to a post and pierce with arrows. Others they compel to extend their necks and then, attacking them with swords, attempt to cut through the neck with a single blow. . . .

Let the deeds of your ancestors move you and incite your minds to manly achievements; the glory and greatness of king Charles the Great, and of his son Louis, and of your other kings, who have destroyed the kingdoms of the pagans, and have extended in these lands the territory of the holy church. Let the holy sepulchre of the Lord our Saviour, which is possessed by unclean nations, especially incite you, and the holy places which are now treated with ignominy and irreverently polluted with their filthiness. Oh, most valiant soldiers and descendants of invincible ancestors, be not degenerate, but recall the valor of your progenitors. . . .

When Pope Urban had said these and very many similar things in his urbane discourse, he so influenced to one purpose the desires of all who were present, that they cried out, "It is the will of God! It is the will of God!" . . .

— 34 —

THE CORONATION OATH OF KING HENRY I, 1100[1]

Henry, the youngest son of the Conqueror, had no reason to expect to become king of England. But his oldest brother, Duke Robert of Normandy, was on his way home from the First Crusade when King William II was killed by an arrow while hunting. Henry was nearby, and when he heard the news dashed to Winchester where lay

[1] Stubbs, *Charters,* p. 99.

the crown and the treasury; he was crowned three days
after the murder. His coronation oath followed the ancient
wording.

In the name of Christ I promise these three things to
the Christian people subject to me. In the first place, I
will devote my rule and power to all men in order that
all Christian people and the church of God may serve the
true peace according to our command for all times;
again, I forbid all rapacity and injustice to all classes of
men; thirdly, I command that there be mercy and fairness
in all judgments, so that a compassionate and clement
God may grant His mercy to me and to you.

— 35 —

THE CORONATION CHARTER OF KING HENRY I, 1101[1]

When Henry succeeded his murdered brother William
II as king, there was some opposition to him, and his
elder brother Duke Robert was alive. This document has
been described as a set of campaign promises, and as such
Henry did not concern himself to carry them out. But
they had been made, and would be resurrected over a
century later, when discontented barons presented John
with the Magna Carta. Henry is willing to limit the
power exercised by William II and his father, and espe-
cially the oppressions of the former. Besides the particular
points, the general appeal is to the "good old days" of
Edward the Confessor, before the church and landowners
had felt the weight of the Norman conquerors.

[1] Stubbs, *Charters*, pp. 100-102.

In the year of the incarnation of the Lord, 1101, Henry, son of King William, after the death of his brother William, by the grace of God, king of the English, to all faithful, greeting:

1. Know that by the mercy of God, and by the common counsel of the barons of the whole kingdom of England, I have been crowned king of this realm; and because the kingdom has been oppressed by unjust exactions, I, out of respect for God, and from the love which I bear towards you, in the first place make the holy church of God free, in such a way that I will neither sell nor lease, nor, at the death of an archbishop, bishop or abbot, will I take anything from the demesne of the church, or from its men, until a successor is installed in it. And I remove all the evil customs by which the kingdom of England has been unjustly oppressed, which evil customs I set down in part here:

2. If any one of my barons, or earls, or others who hold from me shall have died, his heir shall not buy back his land as he did in the time of my brother, but shall relieve it by a just and lawful relief. And, similarly, the men of my barons shall relieve their lands from their lords by a just and lawful relief.

3. And if any one of the barons or other men of mine wishes to give his daughter in marriage, or his sister or niece or relative, he must speak with me about it; but I will neither take any money from him for this permission, nor forbid him to give her, unless he should wish to unite her with my enemy. And if on the death of a baron or other man of mine a daughter should remain as his heir, I will give her in marriage with the counsel of my barons with her land. And if on the death of a man his wife remains and is without children, she shall have her dowry and marriage portion, and I will not give her to a suitor unless according to her wish.

4. And if a wife has survived with children, she will have her dowry and marriage portion so long as she shall protect her person legally, and I will not give her to a suitor unless according to her wish. And the guardian of

the land and the children shall be either the wife or another relative as shall seem more reasonable. And I order that my barons should deal similarly with the sons or daughters or wives of their men.

5. The common tax on money which was taken throughout the cities and counties and which was not taken in the time of King Edward, I now absolutely forbid henceforth to be made. If any one has been seized, whether a moneyer or any other with false money, true justice shall be done for it.

6. I forgive all pleas and all debts that were owed to my brother, except my proper rents, and except those which were stipulated for the inheritance of others, or for those things which more justly concerned others. And if any one for his own inheritance has agreed to anything, this I remit, and all reliefs that had been agreed upon for rightful inheritances.

7. And if any one of my barons or men becomes infirm, since he himself may give or bequeath his money, I grant that it shall be so given. Moreover, if he himself, prevented by war or by infirmity shall not have given his money, or arranged to bequeathe it, his wife or his children or his relatives, or his lawful men shall divide it for his soul, as it may seem best to them.

8. If any of my barons or my men has committed an offence he shall not give a pledge to the extent of his money, as he did in the time of my father or my brother, but according to the kind of the offence so shall he make amends, as was done before my father's time, in the time of my other predecessors. But if he has been convicted of treachery or crime, he shall make amends as is just.

9. I pardon all murders, moreover, before that day on which I was crowned king; and those which shall be done hereafter shall be paid for justly according to the law of King Edward.

10. I have kept the forests in my hands by the common counsel of my barons as my father held them.

11. To the knights who hold their lands by military service armed with a hauberk, I grant of my own gift the lands of their demesne ploughs free from all gelds and from all work in order that just as they have been light-

ened of a great burden, so they may better arrange themselves with horses and arms for my service and for the defense of my kingdom.

12. I place a firm peace on my whole kingdom and order it to be kept henceforth.

13. I restore the law of King Edward to you with those corrections that my father made to it with the counsel of his barons.

14. If anyone has seized anything from my property or from the property of anyone since the death of King William my brother, let all of it be immediately returned without penalty. But if anyone holds back anything, he on whom it may be found will pay heavily to me.

Witnesses.

— 36 —

THE CORONATION CHARTER OF KING STEPHEN, 1135[1]

This document was probably issued by Stephen at his coronation, though this cannot be proved. If he had not been so feckless it would have had considerable importance because of its vague wording. The next year he issued a longer, more precisely worded charter at a large meeting of his court in which he appealed to the clergy for support. But his reign was more fertile for rebels than the issuance of important documents.

       ✓   ✓   ✓

Stephen, by the grace of God, king of the English, to his justices, sheriffs, barons and all his ministers and faithful, both French and English, greeting.

[1] Stubbs, *Charters*, p. 119.

Know that I have granted and by the present charter confirmed to all the barons and my men in England all the liberties and good laws which my uncle, Henry king of the English, gave and conceded to them; and I concede all the good laws and good customs which they had in the time of King Edward.

Wherefore, I will and firmly order that they and their heirs have and hold all those good laws and liberties from me and my heirs freely, peacefully and fully; and I prohibit any one to trouble or obstruct or harm them in these things on pain of forfeiture to me.

Witness, William Martel at London.

— 37 —

THE BULL *LAUDABILITER*, 1155[1]

There have always been, for reasons that should be apparent, those who deny the authenticity of this document. While it cannot be proven genuine, it is established that it expresses papal thoughts on Ireland, and that the papacy was not opposed to the conquest of Ireland by the English. Adrian's mention of papal jurisdiction over Ireland and other islands in the second paragraph is based on the forged Donation of Constantine.

✓   ✓   ✓

Bishop Adrian, servant of the servants of God, sends to his dearest son in Christ, the illustrious king of the English, greeting and apostolic benediction. Laudably and profitably enough thy magnificence thinks of extending thy glorious name on earth, and of heaping up rewards of eternal felicity in Heaven, inasmuch as, like a

[1] Henderson, *Documents,* pp. 10-11.

good catholic prince, thou dost endeavor to enlarge the bounds of the church, to declare the truth of the Christian faith to ignorant and barbarous nations, and to extirpate the plants of evil from the field of the Lord. And, in order the better to perform this, thou dost ask the advice and favor of the apostolic see. In which work, the more lofty the counsel and the better the guidance by which thou dost proceed, so much more do we trust that, by God's help, thou wilt progress favorably in the same; for the reason that those things which have taken their rise from ardor of faith and love of religion are accustomed always to come to a good end and termination.

There is indeed no doubt, as thy Highness doth also acknowledge, that Ireland and all other islands which Christ the Sun of Righteousness has illumined, and which have received the doctrines of the Christian faith, belong to the jurisdiction of St. Peter and of the holy Roman Church. Wherefore, so much the more willingly do we grant to them that the right faith and the seed grateful to God may be planted in them, the more we perceive, by examining more strictly our conscience, that this will be required of us.

Thou hast signified to us, indeed, most beloved son in Christ, that thou dost desire to enter into the island of Ireland, in order to subject the people to the laws and to extirpate the vices that have there taken root, and that thou are willing to pay an annual pension to St. Peter of one penny from every house, and to preserve the rights of the churches in that land inviolate and entire. We, therefore, seconding with the favor it deserves thy pious and laudable desire, and granting a benignant assent to thy petition, are well pleased that, for the enlargement of the bounds of the church, for the restraint of vice, for the correction of morals and the introduction of virtues, for the advancement of the Christian religion, thou should'st enter that island, and carry out there the things that look to the honor of God and to its own salvation. And may the people of that land receive thee with honor, and venerate thee as their master; provided always that the rights of the churches remain inviolate and entire, and saving to St. Peter and the holy Roman Church the annual pension of one penny from each house. If, therefore, thou dost see fit to complete what thou hast conceived in thy mind, strive to imbue that people with good morals, and bring it to pass, as well through thyself as through those whom thou dost know from their faith, doctrine, and course of life to be fit for such a work, that the church may there be adorned, the Christian religion planted and made to grow, and the things which pertain to the honor of God and to salvation be so ordered that thou may'st merit to obtain an abundant and lasting reward from God, and on earth a name glorious throughout the ages.

— 38 —

THE ESTABLISHMENT OF
THE DUCHY OF AUSTRIA, 1156[1]

Prior to 1156 Austria was known as the East Mark and was part of the duchy of Bavaria. At that time, in the presence of Emperor Frederick I, Henry Jasormigott resigned the duchy of Bavaria, which was given to Henry the Lion. But the East Mark was detached from it, raised to a duchy, and given to Henry Jasormigott and his wife. His family of Babenberg held it until 1238, and in 1276 it passed to the Hapsburgs. The great amount of independence granted the new duke is noteworthy. He was the paramount authority and was "a feudal overlord, controlling by feudal ties the nobility within the boundaries of his duchy."

✦   ✦   ✦

In the name of the holy and indivisible Trinity. Frederick, by favor of the divine mercy, august emperor of

[1] Henderson, *Documents,* pp. 215-217.

the Romans. Although a transfer of property may remain valid from the actual act of performing such transfer, and those things which are lawfully possessed can not be wrested away by any act of force; it is, however, the duty of our imperial authority to intervene lest there can be any doubt of the transaction. Be it known, therefore, to the present age and to future generations of our subjects, that we, aided by the grace of Him who sent peace for men from Heaven to earth, have, in the general court of Regensburg which was held on the nativity of St. Mary the Virgin, in the presence of many of the clergy and the catholic princes, terminated the struggle and controversy concerning the duchy of Bavaria, which has long been carried on between our most beloved uncle, Henry duke of Austria, and our most dear nephew, Henry duke of Saxony. And it has been done in this way: that the duke of Austria has resigned to us the duchy of Bavaria, which we have straightway granted as a fief to the duke of Saxony. But the duke of Bavaria has resigned to us the march of Austria, with all its jurisdictions and with all the fiefs which the former margrave Leopold held from the duchy of Bavaria. Moreover, lest by this act the honor and glory of our most beloved uncle may seem in any way to be diminished—by the counsel and judgment of the princes, Vladislav, the illustrious duke of Bohemia, proclaiming the decision, and all the princes approving—we have changed the march of Austria into a duchy, and have granted that duchy with all its jurisdictions to our aforesaid uncle Henry and his most noble wife Theodora as a fief; decreeing by a perpetual law that they and their children alike, whether sons or daughters, shall, by hereditary right, hold and possess that same duchy of Austria from the empire. But if the aforesaid duke of Austria, our uncle, and his wife should die without children, they shall have the privilege of leaving that duchy to whomever they wish. We decree, further, that no person, small or great, may presume to exercise any jurisdiction in the governing of that duchy without the consent or permission of the duke. The duke of Austria, moreover, shall not owe any other service to the empire from his duchy, except that, when he is summoned, he shall come to the courts which the emperor shall announce in Bavaria. And he shall be bound to go on no military expedition, unless the emperor ordain one against the countries or provinces adjoining Austria. For the rest, in order that this our imperial decree may, for all ages, remain valid and unshaken, we have ordered the present charter to be written and to be sealed with the impress of our seal, suitable witnesses to be called in whose names are as follows: Pilgrim, patriarch of Aquileija, etc., etc.

— 39 —

THE CHARTER OBTAINED BY THE CITY OF LINCOLN FROM HENRY II, ca. 1160[1]

Although the liberties obtained by townspeople varied, they usually included a provision that the inhabitants should be free and have some form of self-government. In a sense, merchants were an anachronism in feudal society; they had no status and there was no provision for recognizing them. Charters such as this one provided status and recognition and created a novel type of immunity. The kings and lords who granted them, however, usually found that the proprietary rights they had renounced were more than recompensed by increased revenues from the towns.

✓   ✓   ✓

Henry, by the grace of God, king of England, duke of Normandy and Aquitaine, count of Anjou, to the bishop of Lincoln, justiciars, sheriffs, barons, officers and all his

[1] Univ. of Penn., "Trans. and Rep.," II, 1, pp. 7-8.

faithful, French and English, of Lincoln, greeting. Know
that I have conceded to my citizens of Lincoln all their
liberties and customs and laws, which they had in the
time of Edward and William and Henry, kings of England; and their gild merchant of the men of the city and
of other merchants of the county, just as they had it in the
time of our aforesaid predecessors, kings of England, best
and most freely. And all men who dwell within the four
divisions of the city and attend the market are to be at
the gilds and customs and assizes of the city as they have
been best in the time of Edward, William and Henry,
kings of England. I grant to them moreover, that if anyone shall buy any land within the city, of the burgage of
Lincoln, and shall have held it for a year and a day without any claim, and he who has bought it is able to show
that the claimant has been in the land of England within
the year and has not claimed it, for the future as before
he shall hold it well and in peace, and without any prosecution. I confirm also to them, that if anyone shall have
remained in the city of Lincoln for a year and a day
without claim on the part of any claimant, and has given
the customs, and is able to show by the law and customs
of the city that the claimant has been in existence in the
land of England and has not made a claim against him,
for the future as in the past he shall remain in peace, in
my city of Lincoln, as my citizen. Witnesses, E., bishop
of Lisieux; Thomas, chancellor; H., constable; Henry of
Essex, constable. At Nottingham.

— 40 —

THE CUSTOMS OF NEWCASTLE-UPON-TYNE, TWELFTH CENTURY [1]

This town was founded by Henry I, and this document from the reign of Henry II contains its laws and customs. As was the case with the charter of Louis VI to Lorris, this became the model for charters to other towns. It is apparent that there are a number of situations that the burgesses may deal with, but life was hard for those who did not hold this privileged position. The intent of the king seems to have been less to grant a certain amount of self-government, than to allow the burgesses a slightly freer hand so that they might prosper faster, and thus be able to provide the monarch with more monies.

✶   ✶   ✶

These are the laws and customs which the burgesses of Newcastle-upon-Tyne had in the time of Henry, king of England, and ought to have:

Burgesses may make seizure for debt from those dwelling outside, within their market place and without, and within their house and without, and within their borough and without, without the license of the reeve, unless courts are held in the borough, and unless they are in the army or on guard at the castle.

From a burgess a burgess is not allowed to make seizure for debt without the license of the reeve.

If a burgess has agreed upon anything in the borough with those dwelling outside, the debtor, if he acknowledges it, must pay the debt himself, or he must grant right in the borough.

[1] Univ. of Penn., "Trans. and Rep.," II, 1, pp. 5-6.

Suits which arise in the borough are to be held and finished there, except those which belong to the king's crown.

If any burgess is summoned on any prosecution, he shall not plead outside of the borough except for want of a court. Nor must he respond without day and term, unless he shall have first fallen into an absurd defense; except with regard to things which pertain to the crown.

If a ship has put in at Tynemouth and wishes to depart, it is allowed to the burgesses to buy whatever they wish.

If a suit arises between a burgess and a merchant, it shall be settled before the third tide.

Whatever merchandise a vessel has brought by sea ought to be carried to land, except salt and brine, which ought to be sold on the ship.

If anyone has held land in burgage for a year and a day justly and without persecution, he need not make defense against a claimant, unless the claimant has been outside the realm of England, or in the case where he is a boy having no power to speak.

If a burgess has a son in his house, at his table, the son shall have the same liberty as his father.

If a villain comes to stay in a borough, and there for a year and a day stays as a burgess in the borough, let him remain altogether, unless it has been said beforehand by himself or by his lord that he is to remain for a certain time.

If a burgess makes an accusation concerning any matter, he cannot wage battle against a burgess, but let the burgess defend himself by law, unless it is concerning treason, when he ought to defend himself by battle. Nor can a burgess wage battle against a villain, unless he has first departed from his burgage.

No merchant, unless he is a burgess, may buy any wool, hides, or other merchandise, outside of the town, nor inside of the borough except from burgesses.

If forfeiture happens to a burgess, he shall give six *oras* to the reeve.

In the borough there is no merchet, nor heriot, nor blood fine, nor *stengesdint*.

Each burgess may have his oven and hand-mill if he wishes, saving the king's right to the oven.

If a woman is in transgression concerning bread or concerning ale, no one ought to intermeddle except the reeve. If she shall have transgressed a second time, let her be whipped for her transgression. If for a third time she shall have transgressed, let justice be done upon her.

No one except a burgess may buy clothes for dyeing, nor make, nor shear them.

A burgess may give his land, or sell it, and go whither he wishes, freely and quietly, unless he is engaged in a suit.

— 41 —

THE CONSTITUTIONS OF CLARENDON, 1164 [1]

This document was issued at a meeting of King Henry II's council at Clarendon. It is concerned with immediate problems, but like some other important medieval documents, certain of its paragraphs were to become even more pertinent in the future. Chapter III has a direct bearing on Henry's developing fight with Beckett, who had claimed the year before that clerics could not be sentenced in a secular court. The use of the jury in Chapter VI is the earliest such mention in this type of material.

Moreover, a certain part of the recognized customs and authority of the kingdom is contained in this draft, of which part these are the chapters.

CH. I. If a controversy comes up between laymen, or between laymen and clerics, or between clerics, concern-

[1] Stubbs, *Charters,* pp. 137-140.

ing advowson and presentation of churches, it shall be treated or closed in the court of the lord king.

Ch. II. Churches in the fee of the lord king cannot be given in perpetuity without his assent and permission.

Ch. III. Clerics charged and accused of anything, being summoned by a justice of the king, shall come to his court, to answer there for what it seems to the king's court he should respond to there; and in the ecclesiastical court for what it appears he should respond to there; in such a way that the king's justice shall send to the court of the holy church to see in what manner the matter will be treated there. And if the cleric shall be convicted or shall confess, the church ought not to examine him as for the remainder.

Ch. IV. It is not lawful for archbishops, bishops, and persons of the kingdom to leave the kingdom without the permission of the lord king. And if they go out, if it pleases the lord king, they shall give assurance that neither in going, nor in staying, nor in returning will they seek the hurt or harm of king or kingdom.

Ch. V. The excommunicated should not give a pledge to continue, nor take an oath, but only a pledge and surety of remaining in the judgment of the church so that they may be absolved.

Ch. VI. Laymen shall not be accused unless by true and lawful accusers and witnesses in the presence of the bishop, in such a way that the archdeacon does not lose his right, nor any thing which he ought to have from it. And if those who are complained of are such that no one wishes or dares to accuse them, the sheriff, being requested by the bishop, shall cause twelve lawful men of the neighbourhood or town to swear in the presence of the bishop, that they will discover the truth in the matter, according to their knowledge.

Ch. VII. No man who is a tenant-in-chief of the king, nor any of the ministers on his demesne, shall be excommunicated, nor shall the lands of any one of them be placed under an interdict, unless first the lord king, if he is in the country, or his justiciar if he is outside the kingdom, agrees that justice shall be done to that man: and in such a way that what pertains to the king's court shall be terminated there; and with regard to that which belongs to the ecclesiastical court, it shall be sent thither in order that it may be handled there.

Ch. VIII. Concerning appeals, if they should arise, they should go from the archdeacon to the bishop, from the bishop to the archbishop. And if the archbishop fails to deliver justice, they must come finally to the lord king, in order that by his command the argument may be ended in the court of the archbishop, thus it must not proceed further without the assent of the lord king.

Ch. IX. If a quarrel arises between a cleric and a layman or between a layman and a cleric concerning any tenement which the cleric wants to take as free alms, but the layman as a lay fee: let it be decided by an investigation of twelve lawful men through the judgment of the chief justiciar of the king, in the presence of the justiciar himself, whether the tenement belongs to free alms or to lay fee. And if it is recognized as belonging to free alms the pleading will be in the ecclesiastical court, but if to the lay fee, unless both call to the same bishop or baron, the pleading will be in the king's court. But if, for that fee, both call to the same bishop or baron, the pleading shall be in his court; in such a way that, because of the recognition that was made, he who first was seised shall not lose his seisin, until the case has been proven for the plea.

Ch. X. Anyone in a city or castle or borough or demesne manor of the lord king, if he be summoned by the archdeacon or bishop for some crime for which he ought to answer to them, and he is unwilling to give satisfaction to their summons, may quite permissibly be put under the interdict; but he ought not to be excommunicated until the chief minister of the lord king of that town is summoned in order to compel him by law to come to give satisfaction. And if the minister of the king fails in this matter, he himself shall be at the mercy of the lord king, and the bishop can thereafter restrain the accused by ecclesiastical justice.

Ch. XI. Archbishops, bishops, and all persons of the kingdom who hold from the king in chief have their property of the lord king as a barony, and answer for them to the justices and ministers of the king, and comply with and perform all the royal customs and duties; and, like other barons, they ought to be present with the barons at the judgments of the court of the lord king, until it comes to a judgment leading to loss of life or limb.

CH. XII. When an archbishopric, bishopric, abbey, or priory in the gift of the king is vacant, it ought to be in his hands; and he will thence receive all the revenue and income from it, just as demesne ones. And when it has come to providing for the church, the lord king should summon the more powerful persons of the church, and the election ought to take place in the lord king's own chapel with the assent of the lord king and the counsel of the persons of the kingdom whom he has summoned for this purpose. And there, before he is consecrated, the person elected shall do homage and fealty to the lord king as to his liege lord, for his life and limbs and his earthly honor, saving his order.

CH. XIII. If any of the magnates of the kingdom have prevented an archbishop or bishop or archdeacon from doing justice to himself or his men, the lord king should do justice to them. And if by chance anyone has prevented the lord king his justice, the archbishops, bishops, and archdeacons ought to bring him to justice in order that he may make amends to the lord king.

CH. XIV. Chattels of those in forfeiture of the king may not be detained in a church or churchyard, contrary to the king's justice, because they belong to the king, whether they are found in the churches or outside them.

CH. XV. Pleas concerning debts which are owed either with or without security being placed are in the king's justice.

CH. XVI. The sons of peasants may not be ordained without the consent of the lord on whose land they are known to have been born.

— 42 —

THE ASSIZES OF CLARENDON, 1166[1]

This document reveals many points of fundamental importance in the development of the English constitution. The itinerant justices are put on a more regular basis, and the competence of royal justice is increased. The older methods of compurgation and ordeal may now be supplemented with the reputation and record of the accused (Art. 12). Justice becomes more formal and provision is made (Art. 18) to seek out criminals throughout England. Likewise, juries of presentment are clearly in existence. Art. 21 is interesting in that it indicates that heretics suffer less punishment than those who have broken the forest law.

Here begins the Assize of Clarendon, made by king Henry II, with the approval of the archbishops, bishops, abbots, counts and barons of all England.

1. In the first place the aforesaid king Henry, by the counsel of all his barons, for the preservation of peace and the maintenance of justice, has decreed that an inquest shall be made for each county, and for each hundred by twelve of the more lawful men of the hundred, and by four of the more lawful men of each vill, upon oath that they will speak the truth: whether in their hundred or in their vill there is any man who, since the lord king has been king, has been charged or publicly exposed as being a robber or murderer or thief; or any one who is a concealer of robbers or murderers or thieves. And let the justices inquire into this before them, and the sheriffs before them.

[1] Stubbs, *Documents,* pp. 143-146.

2. And he who is found through the oath of the aforesaid to have been charged or publicly exposed as being a robber or murderer or thief, or a concealer of them, since the lord king has been king, shall be seized and go to the ordeal of water, and shall swear that, to the value of five shillings, so far as he knows, he was not a robber or murderer or thief or concealer of them since the lord king has been king.

3. And if the lord of the man who was seized, or his steward or his men, seek him by pledge within three days after he has been seized, he and his chattels shall be held back under pledge until he has made his law.

4. And when a robber or murderer or thief, or concealers of them, has been seized through the aforesaid oath, if the justices are not to come sufficiently quickly into that county where they have been taken, the sheriffs shall send word to the nearest justice through some knowledgeable man, that they have seized such men; and the justices shall send back word to the sheriffs where they wish those men to be conducted before them: and the sheriffs shall bring them before the justices. And with them they shall bring, from the hundred and vill where they were seized, two lawful men to bring the record for the county and hundred as to why they were seized; and there they will make their law before the justice.

5. And in the case of those who were seized through the aforesaid oath of this Assize, no one shall have court or justice or chattels save the lord king in his court before his justices; and the lord king shall have all their chattels. But in the case of those who shall be seized in another way than by this oath, it shall be as is customary and ought to be.

6. And the sheriffs who seized them shall lead them before the justice without any other summons than they have then. And when the robbers or murderers or thieves, or concealers of them, who shall be seized through the oath or otherwise, are delivered to the sheriffs, they shall receive them immediately without delay.

7. And in those counties where there are no jails, let them be made in a borough or in some castle of the king with the king's money and from his woods if they are near, or from some nearby woods, in view of the king's

servants; to the end that in them the sheriffs may have guarded those who have been seized, by the ministers and their servants who are used to doing this.

8. The lord king wills also that all shall come to the county courts to take this oath; so that no one shall stay away on account of any liberty that he has, or court or soke that he may have, but that they shall come to take this oath.

9. And let there be no one inside or outside his castle, nor even in the honour of Wallingford, who shall forbid the sheriffs to enter into his court or his land to take the view of frankpledge; and let all be under sureties: and let them be sent before the sheriffs under frankpledge.

10. And in the cities or boroughs no one may have men, or receive in his home or on his land or in his soke, those whom he will not take in hand to present before the justice if they be wanted; or are in frankpledge.

11. And no one may be in a city or borough or castle, or outside it, nor also in the honour of Wallingford, who shall forbid the sheriffs to enter into his land or soke to seize those who have been charged or publicly exposed as being robbers or murderers or thieves, or concealers of the same, or outlaws or charged with regard to the forest; the king commands that they shall help the sheriffs seize them.

12. And if anyone shall be seized possessed of robbed or stolen goods, if he has been defamed and has a bad reputation from the public, and has no warranty, he will not have law. And if he is not notorious, on account of the stolen things he has, he shall go to the ordeal by water.

13. And if anyone shall confess before lawful men, or in the hundred court, to robbery or murder or theft, or the concealing of those committing them, and afterwards wants to deny it, he shall not have law.

14. Moreover, the lord king wills also that those who shall be tried and absolved by the law, if they are of very bad repute and are publicly and disgracefully defamed by the testimony of many and lawful men, shall abjure the lands of the king, so that within eight days they shall cross the sea unless the wind detains them; and, with the first wind that they have afterwards, they shall cross the

sea; and they shall not return any more to England unless
by the mercy of the lord king: both there and if they
return, they shall be outlawed; and if they return they
shall be seized as outlaws.

15. And the lord king forbids that any waif, that is, a
vagrant or unknown person, shall be sheltered any where
except in a borough, and there he shall not be sheltered
more than a night, unless he become ill there, or his
horse, so that he can show an obvious excuse.

16. And if he is there more than one night, he shall be
seized and held until his lord shall come to give surety for
him, or until he himself shall procure good sureties; and
likewise he shall be seized who sheltered him.

17. And if any sheriff shall send word to another
sheriff that men have fled his county into another county
on account of robbery or murder or theft, or the concealing of them, or for outlawry, or for an accusation with
regard to the king's forest, he shall seize them: and also
if he knows it of himself or through others that such men
have fled into his county, let him seize them and hold
them in custody until he has good sureties from them.

18. And all sheriffs shall cause a record to be kept of
all fugitives who fled their counties; and they shall do
this in the presence of the county courts; and they shall
carry the names written to the justices when first they
come to them, so that they may be sought for throughout
England, and their chattels may be taken for the use of
the king.

19. And the lord king wills that when the sheriffs receive the summons of the itinerant justices to appear before them with the men of their counties, they shall assemble them and inquire for all who have newly come
into their counties since this assize; and they shall release
them under surety that they come before the justices, or
they shall hold them in custody until the justices come
to them, and then they shall bring them before the justices.

20. Moreover, the lord king forbids monks or canons
or any religious house to receive anyone of the lower
class as monk or canon or brother, until they know of
what reputation he is, unless he is sick unto death.

21. The lord king forbids, moreover, anyone in all

England to receive in his land or his soke or home under him anyone of that sect of renegades who were excommunicated and branded at Oxford. And if anyone receives them, he himself shall be at the mercy of the lord king; and the house in which they have been shall be carried outside the vill and burned. And each sheriff shall swear that he will observe this, and shall make all his ministers swear this, and the stewards of the barons, and all the knights and freeholders of the counties.

22. And the lord king wills that this assize shall be kept in his kingdom as long as it shall please him.

— 43 —

THE *CARTAE BARONUM*, 1166[1]

William the Conqueror established the knight's service owed to him by each of his vassals when they were enfeoffed. In only a few instances was this service changed in the next one hundred years. But how many knights were enfeoffed by these tenants-in-chief? If a tenant-in-chief had enfeoffed more knights than he needed to meet his service, the king could raise the amount; if less, he was still responsible for the service owed. Henry II ordered each of his tenants-in-chief in 1166 to supply him with answers to the questions that appear in the first paragraph of the return supplied by the archbishop of York. The archbishop owed the service of twenty knights, but considerably more had been enfeoffed by himself and his predecessors. Incidentally, without counting the baronies owing less than ten knights, the ecclesiastical ten-

[1] *Liber rubeus de scaccario* (Rolls Series, London, 1896), I, 412-415.

ants-in-chief owed Henry 784 knights, the lay 2140 knights. (J. H. Round, Feudal England (London, 1895), pp. 249-256.)

†   †   †

To his dearest lord, Henry, by the grace of God, king of the English, and duke of the Normans and of the men of Aquitaine, count of the Angevins, his man Roger, by the same grace, archbishop of York, legate of the apostolic see, gives greeting. Your dignity has ordered all your liegemen, cleric and lay, who hold from you in chief in Yorkshire to send to you, by their letters carrying seals outside: how many knights each one has by the old enfeoffment of the time of the king [Henry] your grandfather, that is to say, from the year and the day in which he was alive and dead; and how many knights he has enfeoffed from the new enfeoffment, after the death of your grandfather of good memory. And in this short report there are how many knights' fees there are on the demesne of each, and the names of all these, both of the new and the old enfeoffments, since you want to know if there are any who have not yet done allegiance to you and whose names are not written in your roll, so that they may do allegiance to you before the first Sunday of Lent. I, one of those subject in all things to your orders, have searched with all diligence in my tenement, as the brief time allowed, and in this return declare these things to you, my lord.

In the first place know my lord that there is no knight's fee on the demesne of the archbishopric of York, since we have a sufficient number of enfeoffed knights to perform all the service which we owe you, just as our predecessors did it, and we have even more knights than we owe you as you may learn from the present list. For our predecessors enfeoffed more knights than they owed to the king, not for the necessary service which they owed, but because they wanted to provide for their relatives and servants.

These are the names of those enfeoffed in the time of King Henry [I]. [There follows a list of thirty-nine knights and the service owed. They range from Hugh of Verly who holds a fee of four knights to Leofred who holds a thirteenth part of a knight's fee.]

After the death of King Henry there were enfeoffed:
Peter the butler, half a knight's fee; Peter the chamber-
lain, the twentieth part of a knight's fee; Geoffrey of
Burton, a twelfth of a knight's fee and Gervase of Bretton
a third of a knight's fee.

And since, my lord, I exact from certain of these men
more service than they are now doing, and in truth others
are withholding services which are said to pertain not to
themselves, but to the table and the demesne of the archbishop, I humbly beg that this my return is not able to
harm me or my successors, and that we can recover or
retain the rights of the church. Farewell, my lord. [Added
are seven names, each holding, with one exception, only
fractions of a knights' fee.]

— 44 —

LIST OF PERSONS EXCOMMUNICA-
TED BY ARCHBISHOP THOMAS
BECKET, 1169[1]

*This list reveals in a peculiarly personal way the ex-
tent of Becket's quarrel with King Henry II.*

✓   ✓   ✓

These are the names of those excommunicated by the
lord of Canterbury:

Gilbert, bishop of London and Jocelyn, bishop of Salis-
bury. Geoffrey Ridel, archdeacon of Canterbury; Richard
of Ilchester, archdeacon of Poitiers; Nigel de Sackville;
Richard de Hastings, nephew of Richard de Hastings;

[1] *Materials for the History of Thomas Becket* (Rolls Series,
London, 1882), VI, 601-603.

Letard, nephew of Archbishop Theobald (Becket's predecessor); Robert de Broc; Robert, brother of William of Eynsford; Robert, vicar of Geoffrey, archdeacon of Canterbury; the person who holds the church of Chart; the person who holds the church of Helles; Richard of Luci (justiciar of England); Hugh of St. Clare (earl of Norfolk); Thomas, son of Bernard; Randulf de Broc; William of Ashford; Robert, the butler of Archbishop Theobald; Alan of Ratling; William of Bec.

The person who holds the land of Mundeham, of the manor of Pagham, which the king seized from the church of Canterbury because of John the marshal, if anyone holds it but the king.

The person who holds the land of Lese, of the manor of Otford, which John the brother of William of Eynsford held, if anyone holds it but the king.

John Comyn.

Guy Rufus who holds, like those aforesaid, is to restore whatsoever he received from the revenues of the treasurer of Lisieux to Canterbury.

These are the ones who hold ecclesiastical and lay possessions of the church of Canterbury and of the archbishop of Canterbury, which he wills and demands to be restored to him and his men without diminution. From the bishop of London he demands restored to him whatever he has received from the revenues of his clergy. If there are others who have received ecclesiastical or lay possssions from the hand of the king, or by his grant, belonging to the church of Canterbury, they are excommunicated until they restore these same possessions, and all the things obtained therefrom to the church of Canterbury and the lord archbishop of Canterbury.

In addition, the same archbishop has excommunicated Wimar, who was the clerk of earl Hugh, Adam of Charing and William Giffard.

— 45 —

BULL OF POPE ALEXANDER III ANNOUNCING THE CANONIZATION OF THOMAS BECKET, MARCH 12, 1173[1]

Almost immediately after Becket's murder, miracles were reported by people who had come to his tomb at Canterbury. In a few years it became enormously popular as the goal of a pilgrimage; Chaucer's Canterbury Tales is about one such. As far as the struggle with Henry II was concerned, Becket dead won what Becket alive had not: Henry capitulated completely. His death occurred on December 29 and is commemorated each year.

✓   ✓   ✓

Bishop Alexander, servant of the servants of God, to his beloved sons the prior and monks of the church of Canterbury greeting and apostolic benediction.

The whole body of the faithful must rejoice at the marvels of that saintly and revered man, Thomas, your archbishop. But then you should be filled with still greater joy and exultation, you who have very often gazed with faith at his miracles, and whose church especially deserves to be honored by his most sacred body. We, moreover, having contemplated the fame of the merits by which his life was so wondrously enlightened, not just the universal and celebrated fame of his miracles, but even the testimony in which I have complete confidence of our dear sons, Albert of St. Lawrence in Lucina and

[1] *Materials for the History of Thomas Becket* (Rolls Series, London, 1885), VII, 545-546.

Theodwin of St. Vitalis, cardinal priests and legates of the apostolic see, and of many other people; and having consulted in council with our brethren and a multitude of clergy and laity present in the church, we have solemnly canonized him on Ash Wednesday and decreed that he should be enrolled in the fellowship of holy martyrs. We command, by apostolic authority, that you and the whole body of the faithful in England celebrate his feast each year on the day on which he ended his life by his glorious passion with suitable reverence. Since, therefore, it is right and very fitting for you that his holy body should be buried with the reverence and honor suitable to it, we command you by apostolic rescript to form a solemn procession on some especial day when the clergy and people are assembled, to lay his body devoutly and reverently with respect in the altar, or to place it in some appropriate coffin, as may be convenient, raised above the altar; and to obtain his protection by your devout prayers to God for the salvation of the faithful and the peace of the universal church. Given at Segni, 12 March.

— 46 —

THE FALL OF CONSTANTINOPLE, 1204[1]

The capture of Constantinople by the combined forces of the Venetians and Crusaders meant that the richest city in the Christian world was open to plunder by the victors. The following extract is by a Greek eyewitness, Nicetas.

[1] Univ. of Penn., "Trans. and Rep.," III, 1, pp. 15-16.

Nor can the violation of the Great Church [St. Sophia] be listened to with equanimity. For the sacred altar, formed of all kinds of precious materials and admired by the whole world, was broken into bits and distributed among the soldiers, as was all the other sacred wealth of so great and infinite splendor.

When the sacred vases and utensils of unsurpassable art and grace and rare material, and the fine silver, wrought with gold, which encircled the screen of the tribunal and the ambo, of admirable workmanship, and the door and many other ornaments, were to be borne away as booty, mules and saddled horses were led to the very sanctuary of the temple. Some of these which were unable to keep their footing on the splendid and slippery pavement, were stabbed when they fell, so that the sacred pavement was polluted with blood and filth.

Nay more, a certain harlot, a sharer in their guilt, a minister of the furies, a servant of the demons, a worker of incantations and poisonings, insulting Christ, sat in the patriarch's seat, singing an obscene song and dancing frequently. Nor, indeed, were these crimes committed and others left undone, on the ground that these were of lesser guilt, the others of greater. But with one consent all the most heinous sins and crimes were committed by all with equal zeal. Could those, who showed so great madness against God Himself, have spared the honorable matrons and maidens or the virgins consecrated to God?

— 47 —

THE LOOT TAKEN FROM CONSTANTINOPLE BY ABBOT MARTIN, 1204[1]

One of the participants in the sack of the great city during the Fourth Crusade was Abbot Martin. He was not interested in destroying the statues of classical antiquity and other beautiful works of art as were the crusaders, but in finding relics for his monastery near Paris.

✓   ✓   ✓

. . . In order that the readers' trust in these may be strengthened, we have determined to give a partial list.

First, of the highest importance and worthy of all veneration: A trace of the blood of our Lord Jesus Christ, which was shed for the redemption of all mankind.

Second, a piece of the cross of our Lord on which the Son of the Father, the new Adam, sacrificed for us, paid the debt of the old Adam.

Third, a not inconsiderable piece of St. John, the forerunner of our Lord.

Fourth, the arm of St. James, the Apostle, whose memory is venerated by the whole church.

There were also relics of the other saints, whose names are as follows:

Christopher, the martyr. George, the martyr. Theodore, the martyr. The foot of St. Cosmas, the martyr. Part of the head of Cyprian, the martyr. Pantaleon, the martyr. A tooth of St. Lawrence. Demetrius, the martyr. Stephen, the proto-martyr. Vincentius, Adjutus, Mauritius and his companions. Crisantius and Darius, the martyrs. Gervasius and Protasius, the martyrs. Primus, the martyr.

[1] Univ. of Penn., "Trans. and Rep.," III, 1, pp. 18-19.

Sergius and Bacchus, the martyrs. Protus, the martyr. John and Paul, the martyrs.

Also relics from the following : the place of the Nativity of our Lord; Calvary; our Lord's sepulchre; the stone rolled away; the place of our Lord's ascension; the stone on which John stood when he baptized the Lord; the spot where Christ raised Lazarus; the stone on which Christ was presented in the temple; the stone on which Jacob slept; the stone where Christ fasted; the stone where Christ prayed; the table on which Christ ate the supper; the place where He was captured; the place where the mother of our Lord died; His grave; the grave of St. Peter, the apostle; the relics of the holy apostles, Andrew and Philip; the place where the Lord gave the law to Moses; the holy patriarchs, Abraham, Isaac and Jacob; St. Nicholas, the bishop; Adelasius, the bishop; Agricius, the bishop; John Chrysostom; John, the almsgiver; the milk of the mother of our Lord; Margaret, the virgin; Perpetua, the virgin; Agatha, the virgin; Agnes, the virgin; Lucia, the virgin; Cecilia, the virgin; Adelgundis and Euphemia, the virgins.

— 48 —

THE COMPURGATION OF QUEEN FREDEGONDA, 585[1]

Compurgation was introduced into western Europe by the Germanic tribes. The church adapted the idea when the barbarians were Christianized. Essentially compurgation consisted of a litigant swearing, together with a number of compurgators, often his kinsmen, to the valid-

[1] Univ. of Penn., "Trans. and Rep.," IV, 4, p. 4.

ity of his assertion. It was subject to many abuses and tended to pass out of existence in the thirteenth century.

✦ ✦ ✦

After this the king [Gontran] went to Paris and openly addressed all the people, saying: "My brother Chilperic on his death is said to have left a son, whose governors begged me at the mother's solicitation to stand sponsor for him at the baptismal font on the day of the festival of our Lord's birth; but they did not appear. Next they asked me to have him baptised at Easter, but the child was not brought then. For the third time they prayed me that he might be presented for the sacred rite on St. John's Day, but the child was still kept back. And so they have compelled me to leave home at this disagreeable season of the year. Therefore I have come, and behold, the boy is concealed, he is not shown me. For these reasons I feel certain that matters are not as they have been represented, but that the child is, as I believe, the son of some one of our nobles. For, if it had been of our race, it would have been brought to me. Know, therefore, that I will not acknowledge it until I receive satisfactory proofs of its paternity." When Queen Fredegonda heard this she summoned the chief men of her kingdom, namely, three bishops and three hundred nobles, and with them made oath that Chilperic was the father of the child. By this means suspicion was removed from the king's mind.

— 49 —

THE ORDEAL, TWELTH CENTURY[1]

The ordeal—fire, hot and cold water, hot iron and combat—was an appeal to the judgment of God. The verdict was often absolute, that is to say, in ordeal by combat there was no such thing as being partially defeated: somebody won and somebody lost. On the other hand there was considerable leeway available to those who prescribed an ordeal. The well-known passage on the ordeal by fire of Peter Bartholomew shows some of the possible variants: size of the fire, distance apart of the two piles, speed at which the accused must pass between them. Finally, how long must the person survive the ordeal in order to prove his innocence? Peter lived twelve days, and the crusading army never did agree whether the lance he had found was genuine or not. The first selection is an example for conducting the ordeal of boiling water and is representative of formulae for conducting the other ordeals.

Let the priest go to the church with the prosecutors and with him who is about to be tried. And while the rest wait in the vestibule of the church let the priest enter and put on the sacred garments except the chasuble and, taking the Gospel and the chrismarium and the relics of the saints and the chalice, let him go to the altar and speak thus to all the people standing near: Behold, brethren, the offices of the Christian religion. Behold the law in which is hope and remission of sins, the holy oil of the chrisma, the consecration of the body and blood of our Lord. Look that ye be not deprived of the heritage of such great blessing and of participation in it by implicating yourselves in the crime of another, for it is written, not

[1] Univ. of Penn., "Trans. and Rep.," IV, 4, pp. 7-9.

only are they worthy of death who do these things, but they that have pleasure in them that do them.

Then let him thus address the one who is to undertake the ordeal: I command thee, N., in the presence of all, by the Father, the Son, and the Holy Ghost, by the tremendous day of judgment, by the ministry of baptism, by thy veneration for the saints, that, if thou art guilty of this matter charged against thee, if thou hast done it, or consented to it, or hast knowingly seen the perpetrators of this crime, thou enter not into the church nor mingle in the company of Christians unless thou wilt confess and admit thy guilt before thou art examined in public judgment.

Then he shall designate a spot in the vestibule where the fire is to be made for the water, and shall first sprinkle the place with holy water, and shall also sprinkle the kettle when it is ready to be hung and the water in it, to guard against the illusions of the devil. Then, entering the church with the others, he shall celebrate the ordeal mass. After the celebration let the priest go with the people to the place of the ordeal, the Gospel in his left hand, the cross, censer and relics of the saints being carried ahead, and let him chant the seven penitential psalms with a litany. . . .

[The priest says several prayers and blesses the water.]

Then let the man who is to be tried, as well as the kettle or pot in which is the boiling water, be fumed with the incense of myrrh, and let this prayer be spoken. . . .

Then let the hand that is to be placed in the water be washed with soap and let it be carefully examined whether it be sound; and before it is thrust in let the priest say: I adjure thee, O vessel, by the Father, and the Son, and the Holy Ghost, and by the holy resurrection, and by the tremendous day of judgment, and by the four Evangelists, that if this man be guilty of this crime either by deed or by consent, let the water boil violently, and do thou, O vessel, turn and swing.

After this let the man who is to be tried plunge in his hand, and afterwards let it be immediately sealed up. After the ordeal let him take a drink of holy water. Up to the time of the decision regarding the ordeal (the hand was examined three days later) it is a good thing to mix salt and holy water with all his food and drink.

---

[1] . . . All these things were pleasing to us, and having enjoined on him [i.e., Peter Bartholomew] a fast we declared that a fire should be prepared upon that day on which the Lord was beaten with stripes and put upon the cross for our salvation. And the fourth day thereafter was the day before the Sabbath. So when the appointed day came round a fire was prepared after the noon hour. The leaders and the people to the number of 60,000 came together; the priests were there also with bare feet, clothed in ecclesiastical garments. The fire was made of dry olive branches, covering a space of thirteen feet long; and there were two piles with a space about a foot wide between them. The height of these piles was four feet. Now when the fire had been kindled so that it burned fiercely, I, Raymond, in presence of the whole multitude, spoke: "If Omnipotent God has spoken to this man face to face, and the blessed Andrew has shown him our Lord's lance while he was keeping his vigil, let him go through the fire unharmed. But if it is false, let him be burned together with the lance which he is to carry in his hand." And all responded on bended knees, "Amen." The fire was growing so hot that the flames shot up thirty cubits high into the air and scarcely any one dared approach it. Then Peter Bartholomew clothed only in his tunic and kneeling before the bishop of Albar called God to witness "that he had seen Him face to face on the cross, and that he had heard from Him those things above written. . . ." Then when the bishop had placed the lance in his hand, he kneeled and made the sign of the cross and entered the fire with the lance, firm and unterrified. For an instant's time he paused in the midst of the flames, and then by the grace of God passed through. . . . But when Peter emerged from the fire so that neither his tunic was burned nor even the thin cloth with which the lance was wrapped up had shown any signs of damage, the whole people received him after that he had made over them the

[1] *Ibid.*, pp. 14-15.

sign of the cross with the lance in his hand and had cried,
"God aid us !" All the people, I say, threw themselves
upon him and dragged him to the ground and trampled
on him, each one wishing to touch him or to get a piece
of his garment, and each thinking him near someone
else. And so he received three or four wounds in the legs
where the flesh was torn away, his back was injured and
his sides bruised. Peter had died on the spot, as we believe, had not Raimond Pelet, a brave and noble soldier,
broken through the wild crowd with a band of friends
and rescued him at the peril of their lives. . . . After this
(twelve days later) Peter died in peace at the hour appointed to him by God, and journeyed to the Lord; and
he was buried in the place where he had carried the lance
of the Lord through the fire.

— 50 —

INTERROGATION OF ALBIGENSIANS[1]

*Bernard Gui became bishop of Tuy in Galicia in 1323,
but he continued as an Inquisitor and found little time to
visit his diocese. He wrote a manual on the conduct of
the Inquisition, and the following selection is the form for
interrogating Albigensians. These heretics flourished especially in Southern France and were the victims of a
crusade.*

The prisoner is first asked if he has seen or known anywhere one or more heretics, whether he knows or believes
them to be such by name or by reputation, where he has

[1] Bernard Gui, *Manuel de l'Inquisiteur, Les Classiques de
l'Histoire de France au Moyen Age* (Paris, 1926), I, 26-
32.

seen them, how many times, with whom and when;

Item, If he has had any close friendship with them, when and how, and who arranged it for them.

Item, If he has received in his house one or more heretics, who and which ones; who brought them to him; how many times they were there; who called on them there; who took them away, where they went.

Item, If he has heard their preaching and what they said and taught.

Item, If he worshipped them, if he saw other people worship them or do reverence to them in the heretical fashion and how was it done.

Item, If he has eaten bread blessed by them and what the manner of blessing the bread was.

Item, If he concluded with them the agreement, by which he wanted to be received, at death's door, in their sect and in their order.

Item, If he greeted them or saw other people greet them in the heretical way, that is by placing the hands on the two cheeks of the heretic, lowering the head and turning it alternately towards the two cheeks and repeating three times: *"Benedicite"*; this is the manner of greeting of the believers who have become "perfecti" when they arrive and depart.

Item, If he took part in the initiation of one of them; how it was conducted; what was the name of the heretic or heretics, those present, the location of the house where the sick person lay, the length of the ceremony, the hour at which it was held; if the initiate had bequeathed something to the heretics, what and how much, who paid the bequest; if prayers were said to the new heretic; if the initiate had died of the sickness and where he was buried; who brought and took away from the house the heretic or heretics.

Item, If he thought that the person initiated into the heretic's faith could be saved.

Item, What the heretics taught and believed in his presence against the faith and the sacraments of the Roman church; what he had heard them say of the sacrament of the Eucharist, baptism, marriage, about the confession of sins to priests, of the adoration or veneration of the Holy Cross and the other errors exposed above.

Item, If he thought that the heretics were good, sincere men, having and holding a true faith, and had a moral sect, correct doctrine, and that they could save themselves and other believers in their faith and their sect;

Item, How long he had held or maintained this belief.

Item, When he had begun to believe it.

Item, If he still believed it.

Item, When and why he withdrew from it.

Item, If he had been called or summoned previously before any inquisitor, when and why; if he had made any confession about heresy, if he had abjured his error in the presence of an inquisitor and if he had been reconciled or absolved.

Item, If since then he had committed any heretical act, what one and how, as above.

Item, If he knew one or more believers sharing heretical feelings or sheltering them.

Item, If he had accompanied sometimes one or more heretics from one place to another, or if he had any of their books.

Item, If his parents had been believers, or agreed to the heresy or had performed penances because of their heresy.

These are the general questions for this sect from which by the prudent zeal and skill of the inquisitor particular points frequently would be developed.

— 51 —

THE SPECIAL OATH TAKEN BY THE WALDENSIANS TO DISAVOW THEIR SECT[1]

The Waldensians, founded about 1174 by Peter Waldo, a merchant of Lyons, were persecuted for heretical beliefs. They somehow survived and a Waldensian Church is still in existence in northwest Italy. The Inquisition provided a special form for those wishing to abjure each heresy, the following is that used for the Waldensians.

I ——————— of ———————, in the diocese of ——————— placed in judgment before you ——— ———, Inquisitor, in the presence of the most holy Gospels of God, completely abjure all heresy contrary to the faith of our Lord Jesus Christ and the Holy Roman Church, and particularly the sect and heresy called Waldensian or the Poor of Lyons, with which I have had dealings and taken part in, whose errors I believed and whose statements I thought true; I renounce especially this error ——————— I disavow all their doctrine; I no longer want to be among their partisans, defenders, shelterers or partake of them under the penalty inflicted by law on relapsed heretics who have abjured a heresy in court.

Item, I swear and promise, insofar as I am able, to pursue, to discover, to denounce and to have seized and brought to the inquisitors heretics and especially the Waldensians and their believers* and also those whom I know or believe to have fled because of heresy; including

[1] Bernard Gui, *Manuel de l'Inquisiteur, Les Classiques de l'Histoire de France au Moyen Age* (Paris, 1927), II, 34-36; from * to end, p. 28.

the aforesaid and even their messengers, at all times and everywhere that I know they might be.

Item, I swear and promise to hold, practice and defend the Catholic faith that the Roman church teaches and observes.

Item, I promise and swear to obey and abide by the mandates of the church and its inquisitors, to come before them or their assigns on the days appointed, when and as often as I may be required or demanded by their messenger, by letter or otherwise; never to flee or knowingly and contumaciously not present myself, to accept and perform as far as I am able the punishment or penance that may be imposed on me.

I obligate myself and encumber all my possessions to the execution of this oath.

— 52 —

CANONS OF THE FOURTH LATERAN COUNCIL DEALING WITH HERESY, 1215[1]

3. . . . Convicted heretics shall be handed over for due punishment to their secular superiors, of the latter's agents. If they are clerks, they shall first be degraded. The goods of the laymen thus convicted shall be confiscated: those of the clergy shall be applied to the churches from which they drew their stipends.

[1] *Decrees of the Fourth Lateran Council, 1215,* as trans. in Henry Bettenson, *Documents of the Christian Church* (Oxford University Press, London, 1946), pp. 185-186.

. . . If a temporal lord neglects to fulfil the demand of the church that he shall purge his land of this contamination of heresy, he shall be excommunicated by the metropolitan and other bishops of the province. If he fails to make amends within a year, it shall be reported to the Supreme Pontiff, who shall pronounce his vassals absolved from fealty to him and offer his land to Catholics. The latter shall exterminate the heretics, possess the land without dispute and preserve it in the true faith. . . .

Catholics who assume the cross and devote themselves to the extermination of heretics shall enjoy the same indulgence and privilege as those who go to the Holy Land. . . .

7. Further we add that every archbishop and bishop, in person or by his archdeacon or other suitable and trustworthy persons, shall visit each of his parishes, in which there are said to be heretics, twice or at least once a year. And he shall compel three or more men of good reputation, or even, if need be, the whole neighborhood, to swear that, if any of them knows of any heretics or of any who frequent secret conventicles or who practice manners and customs different from those common amongst Christians, he will report them to the bishop. The bishop shall summon those accused to appear before him; and, unless they clear themselves of the accusation, or if they relapse into their former mischief, they shall receive canonical punishment. . . .

— 53 —

ST. THOMAS AQUINAS (1225-1274) ON THE INQUISITION[1]

ARTICLE III. *Whether heretics should be tolerated.*

I reply that, with regard to heretics, two considerations are to be kept in mind: (1) on their side, (2) on the side of the Church.

(1) There is the sin, whereby they deserve not only to be separated from the Church by excommunication, but also to be shut off from the world by death. For it is a much more serious matter to corrupt faith, through which comes the soul's life, than to forge money, through which temporal life is supported. Hence if forgers of money or other malefactors are straightway justly put to death by secular princes, with much more justice can heretics, immediately upon conviction, be not only excommunicated but also put to death.

(2) But on the side of the Church there is mercy, with a view to the conversion of them that are in error; and therefore the Church does not straightway condemn, but *after a first and a second admonition,* as the Apostle teaches (*Tit.* iii. 10). After that, if he be found still stubborn, the Church gives up hope of his conversion and takes thought for the safety of others, by separating him from the Church by sentence of excommunication; and, further, leaves him to the secular court, to be exterminated from the world by death. . . .

---

[1] From *Summa Theologica,* ii, Q. xi. Art. iii, in Bettenson, *Documents of the Christian Church* (London, 1946), pp. 186-187.

— 54 —

FRANCE IS PLACED UNDER THE INTERDICT BY INNOCENT III, 1200[1]

The reason for this interdict was the refusal by King Philip II Augustus of France to put aside Agnes of Meran for his wife Ingeburg of Denmark whom he had married and separated from in 1193. Philip finally yielded in March, 1201, to the demands of the pope, but in form only. The awful power of the interdict is clearly shown in this example. Even confession is for all practical purposes prohibited. In effect, the interdict accomplished for a territory what excommunication did for an individual. "France" is Philip's realm, not the present nation.

✓   ✓   ✓

Let all the churches be closed; let no one be admitted to them except to baptize infants; let them not be otherwise opened except for the purpose of lighting the lamps, or when the priest shall come for the Eucharist and holy water for the use of the sick. We permit mass to be celebrated once a week on Friday early in the morning to consecrate the Host for the use of the sick, but only one clerk is to be admitted to assist the priest. Let the clergy preach on Sunday in the vestibules of the churches, and in place of the mass let them disseminate the word of God. Let them recite the canonical hours outside the churches, where the people do not hear them; if they recite an epistle or a gospel let them beware lest the laity hear them; and let them not permit the dead to be interred, or their bodies to be placed unburied in the cemeteries. Let them, moreover, say to the laity that they sin

[1] Univ. of Penn., "Trans. and Repr.," IV, 3, pp. 29-30.

and transgress grievously by burying bodies in the earth, even in unconsecrated ground, for in so doing they arrogate to themselves an office pertaining to others. Let them forbid their parishioners to enter churches that may be open in the king's territory, and let them not bless the wallets of pilgrims except outside the churches. Let them not celebrate the offices in Passion week, but refrain even till Easter day, and then let them celebrate in private, no one being admitted except the assisting priest, as above directed; let no one communicate even at Easter, except he be sick and in danger of death. During the same week, or on Palm Sunday, let them announce to their parishioners that they may assemble on Easter morning before the church and there have permission to eat flesh and consecrated bread. Women are expressly forbidden to be admitted into the churches for purification, but are to be warned to gather their neighbors together on the day of purification and pray outside the church, nor may the women who are to be purified enter even to raise their children to the sacred font for baptism until they are admitted by the priest after the expiration of the interdict. Let the priest confess all who desire it in the portico of the church; if the church have no portico we direct that in bad or rainy weather, and not otherwise, the nearest door of the church may be opened and confessions heard on its threshold (all being excluded except the one who is to confess) so that the priest and the penitent can be heard by those who are outside the church. If, however, the weather be fair, let the confession be heard in front of the closed doors. Let no vessels of holy water be placed outside of the church, nor shall the priests carry them anywhere, for all the sacraments of the church beyond these two which were reserved are absolutely prohibited. Extreme unction, which is a holy sacrament, may not be given.

— 55 —

KING JOHN SUBMITS TO POPE INNOCENT III, 1213[1]

By the following letter John handed over England and Ireland as fiefs to Innocent and his successors and agreed to an annual payment of 1000 marks. The pope was already recognized as the overlord of Sicily, Aragon, Portugal, and Hungary among other places. Of all the medieval popes, Innocent was the most successful in claiming that the souls of kings were in his care as the vicar of God. Be that as it may, John was no longer excommunicated, nor was England under the interdict, and he had forestalled the rebellious baronage who hesitated to attack a vassal of the pope.

✓   ✓   ✓

John, by the grace of God king of England, lord of Ireland, duke of Normandy and Aquitaine, count of Anjou, to all the faithful of Christ who may see this charter, greeting in the Lord.

By this charter attested by our golden seal we wish it to be known to you all that, having in many things offended God and Holy Church our mother and being therefore in the utmost need of divine mercy and possessing nothing but ourselves and our kingdoms that we can worthily offer as due amends to God and the Church, we desire to humble ourselves for the sake of Him who for us humbled Himself even unto death; and inspired by the grace of the Holy Spirit—not induced by force nor compelled by fear, but of our own good and spontaneous

[1] Cheney and Semple (ed.), *Selected Letters of Pope Innocent III* (Thomas Nelson and Sons, Ltd., London, 1953), pp. 178-181.

will and on the general advice of our barons—we offer
and freely yield to God, and to SS. Peter and Paul His
apostles, and to the Holy Roman Church our mother, and
to our lord Pope Innocent III and his catholic successors,
the whole kingdom of England and the whole kingdom of
Ireland with all their rights and appurtenances for the
remission of our sins and the sins of our whole family,
both the living and the dead. And now, receiving back
these kingdoms from God and the Roman Church and
holding them as feudatory vassal, in the presence of our
venerable father, lord Nicholas, bishop of Tusculum, legate of the Apostolic See, and of Pandulf, subdeacon and
member of household to our lord the Pope, we have
pledged and sworn our fealty henceforth to our lord
aforesaid, Pope Innocent, and to his catholic successors,
and to the Roman Church, in the terms hereinunder
stated; and we have publicly paid liege homage for the
said kingdoms, and to the Holy Apostles Peter
and Paul, and to the Roman Church, and to our lord
aforesaid, Pope Innocent III, at the hands of the said
legate who accepts our homage in place and instead of
our said lord, the Pope; and we bind in perpetuity our
successors and legitimate heirs that without question they
must similarly render fealty and acknowledge homage to
the Supreme Pontiff holding office at the time and to the
Roman Church. As a token of this our perpetual offering
and concession we will and decree that out of the proper
and special revenues of our said kingdoms, in lieu of all
service and payment which we should render for them, the
Roman Church is to receive annually, without prejudice
to the payment of Peter's pence, one thousand marks
sterling—five hundred at the feast of St. Michael and
five hundred at Easter—that is, seven hundred for the
kingdom of England and three hundred for the kingdom
of Ireland, subject to the maintenance for us and our
heirs of our jurisdiction, privileges, and regalities. De-
siring all these terms, exactly as stated, to be forever
ratified and valid, we bind ourselves and our successors
not to contravene them; and if we or any of our successors shall presume to contravene them, then, no matter
who he be, unless on due warning he come to his senses,
let him lose the title to the kingdom, and let this document

of our offer and concession remain ever valid. [The next paragraph is John's oath.]

I, John, by grace of God king of England and lord of Ireland, will from this hour henceforward be faithful to God and Saint Peter and the Roman Church and my lord Pope Innocent III and his catholic successors. I will not take part in deed, word, agreement, or plan whereby they should lose life or limb or be treacherously taken prisoners; any injury to them, if aware of it, I will prevent and will check if I can; and otherwise, I will notify them as soon as possible, or inform a person whom I can trust without fail to tell them; any counsel they have entrusted to me either personally or by envoys or by letter I will keep secret, nor will I wittingly divulge it to anyone to their disadvantage. I will help in maintaining and defending, to the utmost of my power, against all men, the patrimony of Saint Peter, and particularly the kingdom of England and the kingdom of Ireland. So help me God and the Holy Gospels of God whereon I swear.

To prevent any questioning of these terms at any time in the future, and for the greater surety of our offer and concession, we have caused this charter to be made and to be sealed with our golden seal; and as tribute for this the first year we pay a thousand marks sterling to the Roman Church by the hand of the said legate.

Witnessed by [the names follow].

— 56 —

MAGNA CARTA, 1215[1]

The importance of this document was expressed by Bishop Stubbs when he wrote that "The whole of the

[1] Henderson, *Documents*, pp. 135-148.

*Constitutional History of England is a commentary on
this charter." It was reissued in 1216 and 1217 and finally
the reissue of 1225, with the accumulated changes that
had been made, became the official version of ensuing
reigns. It was annulled within three months by John's
lord, Innocent III, but he could not defeat the concept
that a king was bound by law. While the "freeman" of
Art. 39 is usually held to mean a baron, the idea slowly
developed that this document provided fundamental rights
for all people and not one class.*

✓   ✓   ✓

John, by the grace of God king of England, lord of
Ireland, duke of Normandy and Aquitaine, count of
Anjou: to the archbishops, bishops, abbots, earls, barons,
justices, foresters, sheriffs, prevosts, serving men, and to
all his bailiffs and faithful subjects, greeting. Know that
we, by the will of God and for the safety of our soul, and
of the souls of all our predecessors and our heirs, to the
honor of God and for the exalting of the holy church and
the bettering of our realm: by the counsel of our venerable
fathers . . . and others of our faithful subjects:

1. First of all have granted to God, and, for us and for
our heirs forever, have confirmed, by this our present
charter, that the English church shall be free and shall
have its rights intact and its liberties uninfringed upon.
And thus we will that it be observed. As is apparent from
the fact that we, spontaneously and of our own free will,
before discord broke out between ourselves and our barons, did grant and by our charter confirm—and did cause
the lord pope Innocent III to confirm—freedom of elections, which is considered most important and most necessary to the church of England. Which charter both we
ourselves shall observe, and we will that it be observed
with good faith by our heirs forever. We have also
granted to all free men of our realm, on the part of ourselves and our heirs forever, all the subjoined liberties,
to have and to hold, to them and to their heirs, from us
and from our heirs:

2. If any one of our earls or barons, or of others holding from us in chief through military service, shall die;
and if, at the time of his death, his heir be of full age and

owe a relief: he shall have his inheritance by paying the old relief;—the heir, namely, or the heirs of an earl, by paying one hundred pounds for the whole barony of an earl; the heir or heirs of a baron, by paying one hundred pounds for the whole barony; the heir or heirs of a knight, by paying one hundred shillings at most for a whole knight's fee; and he who shall owe less shall give less, according to the ancient custom of fees.

3. But if the heir of any of the above persons shall be under age and in wardship,—when he comes of age he shall have his inheritance without relief and without fine.

4. The administrator of the land of such heir who shall be under age shall take none but reasonable issues from the land of the heir, and reasonable customs and services; and this without destruction and waste of men or goods. And if we shall have committed the custody of any such land to the sheriff or to any other man who ought to be responsible for us for the issues of it, and he cause destruction or waste to what is in his charge: we will fine him, and the land shall be handed over to two lawful and discreet men of that fee who shall answer to us, or to him to whom we shall have referred them, regarding those issues. And if we shall have given or sold to any one the custody of any such land, and he shall have caused destruction or waste to it,—he shall lose that custody, and it shall be given to two lawful and discreet men of that fee, who likewise shall answer to us, as has been explained.

5. The administrator, moreover, so long as he may have the custody of the land, shall keep in order, from the issues of that land, the houses, parks, warrens, lakes, mills, and other things pertaining to it. And he shall restore to the heir when he comes to full age, his whole land stocked with ploughs and wainnages, according as the time of the wainnage requires and the issues of the land will reasonably permit.

6. Heirs may marry without disparagement; so, nevertheless, that, before the marriage is contracted, it shall be announced to the relations by blood of the heir himself.

7. A widow, after the death of her husband, shall straightway, and without difficulty, have her marriage portion and her inheritance, nor shall she give any thing

in return for her dowry, her marriage portion, or the inheritance which belonged to her, and which she and her husband held on the day of the death of that husband. And she may remain in the house of her husband, after his death, for forty days; within which her dowry shall be paid over to her.

8. No widow shall be forced to marry when she prefers to live without a husband; so, however, that she gives security not to marry without our consent, if she hold from us, or the consent of the lord from whom she holds, if she hold from another.

9. Neither we nor our bailiffs shall seize any revenue for any debt, so long as the chattels of the debtor suffice to pay the debt; nor shall the sponsors of that debtor be distrained so long as that chief debtor has enough to pay the debt. But if the chief debtor fail in paying the debt, not having the wherewithal to pay it, the sponsors shall answer for the debt. And, if they shall wish, they may have the lands and revenues of the debtor until satisfaction shall have been given them for the debt previously paid for him; unless the chief debtor shall show that he is quit in that respect towards those same sponsors. . . .

[Articles 10 and 11 deal with debts to the Jews.]

12. No scutage or aid shall be imposed in our realm unless by the common counsel of our realm; except for redeeming our body, and knighting our eldest son, and marrying once our eldest daughter. And for these purposes there shall only be given a reasonable aid. In like manner shall be done concerning the aids of the city of London.

13. And the city of London shall have all its old liberties and free customs as well by land as by water. Moreover we will and grant that all other cities and burroughs, and towns and ports, shall have all their liberties and free customs.

14. And, in order to have the common counsel of the realm in the matter of assessing an aid otherwise than in the aforesaid cases, or of assessing a scutage,—we shall cause, under seal through our letters, the archbishops, bishops, abbots, earls, and greater barons to be summoned for a fixed day—for a term, namely, at least forty days

distant,—and for a fixed place. And, moreover, we shall cause to be summoned in general, through our sheriffs and bailiffs, all those who hold of us in chief. And in all those letters of summons we shall express the cause of the summons. And when a summons has thus been made, the business shall be proceeded with on the day appointed according to the counsel of those who shall be present, even though not all shall come who were summoned.

15. We will not allow anyone henceforth to take an aid from his freemen save for the redemption of his body, and the knighting of his eldest son, and the marrying, once, of his eldest daughter; and, for these purposes, there shall only be given a reasonable aid.

16. No one shall be forced to do more service for a knight's fee, or for another free holding, than is due from it.

17. Common pleas shall not follow our court but shall be held in a certain fixed place.

18. Assizes of novel disseisin, of mort d'ancester, and of darrein presentment shall not be held save in their own counties, and in this way: we, or our chief justice, if we shall be absent from the kingdom, shall send two justices through each county four times a year; they, with four knights from each county, chosen by the county, shall hold the aforesaid assizes in the county, and on the day and at the place of the county court.

19. And if on the day of the county court the aforesaid assizes can not be held, a sufficient number of knights and free tenants, from those who were present at the county court on that day, shall remain, so that through them the judgments may be suitably given, according as the matter may have been great or small.

20. A freeman shall only be amerced for a small offence according to the measure of that offence. And for a great offence he shall be amerced according to the magnitude of the offence, saving his contenement; and a merchant, in the same way, saving his merchandise. And a villein, in the same way, if he fall under our mercy, shall be amerced saving his wainnage. And none of the aforesaid fines shall be imposed save upon oath of upright men from the neighborhood.

21. Earls and barons shall not be amerced save through their peers, and only according to the measure of the offence.

22. No clerk shall be amerced for his lay tenement except according to the manner of the other persons aforesaid; and not according to the amount of his ecclesiastical benefice.

23. Neither a town nor a man shall be forced to make bridges over the rivers, with the exception of those who, from of old and of right, ought to do it.

24. No sheriff, constable, coroners, or other bailiffs of ours shall hold the pleas of our crown.

25. All counties, hundreds, wapentakes, and trithings—our demesne manors being excepted—shall continue according to the old farms, without any increase at all.

26. If anyone holding from us a lay fee shall die, and our sheriff or bailiff can show our letters patent containing our summons for the debt which the dead man owed to us,—our sheriff or bailiff may be allowed to attach and enroll the chattels of the dead man to the value of that debt, through view of lawful men; in such way, however, that nothing shall be removed thence until the debt is paid which was plainly owed to us. And the residue shall be left to the executors that they may carry out the will of the dead man. And if nothing is owed to us by him, all the chattels shall go to the use prescribed by the deceased, saving their reasonable portions to his wife and children.

27. If any freeman shall have died intestate his chattels shall be distributed through the hands of his near relatives and friends, by view of the church; saving to anyone the debts which the dead man owed him.

28. No constable or other bailiff of ours shall take the corn or other chattels of anyone except he straightway give money for them, or can be allowed a respite in that regard by the will of the seller.

29. No constable shall force any knight to pay money for castleward if he be willing to perform that ward in person, or—he for a reasonable cause not being able to perform it himself—through another proper man. And if we shall have led or sent him on a military expedition, he shall be quit of ward according to the amount of time

during which, through us, he shall have been in military service.

30. No sheriff nor bailiff of ours, nor anyone else, shall take the horses or carts of any freeman for transport, unless by the will of that freeman.

31. Neither we nor our bailiffs shall take another's wood for castles or for other private uses, unless by the will of him to whom the wood belongs.

32. We shall not hold the lands of those convicted of felony longer than a year and a day; and then the lands shall be restored to the lords of the fiefs.

33. Henceforth all the weirs in the Thames and Medway, and throughout all England, save on the sea-coast, shall be done away with entirely.

34. Henceforth the writ which is called *Praecipe* shall not be served on anyone for any holding so as to cause a free man to lose his court.

35. There shall be one measure of wine throughout our whole realm, and one measure of ale and one measure of corn—namely, the London quart;—and one width of dyed and russet and hauberk cloths—namely, two ells below the selvage. And with weights, moreover, it shall be as with measures.

36. Henceforth nothing shall be given or taken for a writ of inquest in a matter concerning life or limb; but it shall be conceded gratis, and shall not be denied.

37. If anyone hold of us in fee-farm, or in socage, or in burkage, and hold land of another by military service, we shall not, by reason of that fee-farm, or socage, or burkage, have the wardship of his heir or of his land which is held in fee from another. Nor shall we have the wardship of that fee-farm, or socage, or burkage unless that fee-farm owe military service. We shall not, by reason of some petit-serjeanty which someone holds of us through the service of giving us knives or arrows or the like, have the wardship of his heir or of the land which he holds of another by military service.

38. No bailiff, on his own simple assertion, shall henceforth put anyone to his law, without producing faithful witnesses in evidence.

39. No freeman shall be taken, or imprisoned, or disseized, or outlawed, or exiled, or in any way harmed—

nor will we go upon or send upon him—save by the lawful judgment of his peers or by the law of the land.

40. To none will we sell, to none deny or delay, right or justice.

41. All merchants may safely and securely go out of England, and come into England, and delay and pass through England, as well by land as by water, for the purpose of buying and selling, free from all evil taxes, subject to the ancient and right customs—save in time of war, and if they are of the land at war against us. And if such be found in our land at the beginning of the war, they shall be held, without harm to their bodies and goods, until it shall be known to us or our chief justice how the merchants of our land are to be treated who shall, at that time, be found in the land at war against us. And if ours shall be safe there, the others shall be safe in our land.

42. Henceforth any person, saving fealty to us, may go out of our realm and return to it, safely and securely, by land and by water, except perhaps for a brief period in time of war, for the common good of the realm. But prisoners and outlaws are excepted according to the law of the realm; also people of a land at war against us, and the merchants, with regard to whom shall be done as we have said.

43. If anyone hold from any escheat—as from the honor of Wallingford, Nottingham, Boloin, Lancaster, or the other escheats which are in our hands and are baronies—and shall die, his heir shall not give another relief, nor shall he perform for us other service than he would perform for a baron if that barony were in the hand of a baron; and we shall hold it in the same way in which the baron has held it.

44. Persons dwelling without the forest shall not henceforth come before the forest justices, through common summonses, unless they are impleaded or are the sponsors of some person or persons attached for matters concerning the forest.

45. We will not make men justices, constables, sheriffs, or bailiffs, unless they are such as know the law of the realm, and are minded to observe it rightly.

46. All barons who have founded abbeys for which they

have charters of the kings of England, or ancient right of tenure, shall have, as they ought to have, their custody when vacant.

47. All forests constituted as such in our time shall straightway be annulled; and the same shall be done for river banks made into places of defence by us in our time.

48. All evil customs concerning forests and warrens, and concerning foresters and warreners, sheriffs and their servants, river banks and their guardians, shall straightway be inquired into in each county, through twelve sworn knights from that county, and shall be eradicated by them, entirely, so that they shall never be renewed, within forty days after the inquest has been made; in such manner that we shall first know about them, or our justice if we be not in England.

49. We shall straightway return all hostages and charters which were delivered to us by Englishmen as a surety for peace or faithful service.

50. We shall entirely remove from their bailiwicks the relatives of Gerard de Athyes, so that they shall henceforth have no bailiwick in England: Engelard de Cygnes, Andrew Peter and Gyon de Chanceles, Gyon de Cygnes, Geoffrey de Martin and his brothers, Philip Mark and his brothers, and Geoffrey his nephew, and the whole following of them.

51. And straightway after peace is restored we shall remove from the realm all the foreign soldiers, crossbowmen, servants, hirelings, who may have come with horses and arms to the harm of the realm.

52. If anyone shall have been disseized by us, or removed, without a legal sentence of his peers, from his lands, castles, liberties or lawful right, we shall straightway restore them to him. And if a dispute shall arise concerning this matter it shall be settled according to the judgment of the twenty-five barons who are mentioned below as sureties for the peace. But with regard to all those things of which anyone was, by king Henry our father or king Richard our brother, disseized or dispossessed without legal judgment of his peers, which we have in our hand or which others hold, and for which we ought to give a guarantee: we shall have respite until the common term for crusaders. Except with regard to

those concerning which a plea was moved, or an inquest made by our order, before we took the cross. But when we return from our pilgrimage, or if, by chance, we desist from our pilgrimage, we shall straightway then show full justice regarding them.

53. We shall have the same respite, moreover, and in the same manner, in the matter of showing justice with regard to forests to be annulled and forests to remain, which Henry our father or Richard our brother constituted; and in the matter of wardships of lands which belong to the fee of another—wardships of which kind we have hitherto enjoyed by reason of the fee which some one held from us in military service;—and in the matter of abbeys founded in the fee of another than ourselves—in which the lord of the fee may say that he has jurisdiction. And when we return, or if we desist from our pilgrimage, we shall straightway exhibit full justice to those complaining with regard to these matters.

54. No one shall be taken or imprisoned on account of the appeal of a woman concerning the death of another than her husband.

55. All fines imposed by us unjustly and contrary to the law of the land, and all amerciaments made unjustly and contrary to the law of the land, shall be altogether remitted, or it shall be done with regard to them according to the judgment of the twenty barons mentioned below as sureties for the peace, or according to the judgment of the majority of them together with the aforesaid Stephen archbishop of Canterbury, if he can be present, and with others whom he may wish to associate with himself for this purpose. And if he cannot be present, the affair shall nevertheless proceed without him; in such way that, if one or more of the said twenty-five barons shall be concerned in a similar complaint, they shall be removed as to this particular decision, and, in their place, for this purpose alone, others shall be substituted who shall be chosen and sworn by the remainder of those twenty-five.

[Articles 56, 57, and 58 concern the Welsh.]

59. We shall act towards Alexander king of the Scots regarding the restoration of his sisters, and his hostages, and his liberties and his lawful right, as we shall act towards our other barons of England; unless it ought to

be otherwise according to the charters which we hold from William, his father, the former king of the Scots. And this shall be done through judgment of his peers in our court.

60. Moreover all the subjects of our realm, clergy as well as laity, shall, as far as pertains to them, observe, with regard to their vassals, all these aforesaid customs and liberties which we have decreed shall, as far as pertains to us, be observed in our realm with regard to our own.

61. [Contains elaborate provisions to enforce the charter.]

62. And we have fully remitted to all, and pardoned, all the ill-will, anger and rancour which have arisen between us and our subjects, clergy and laity, from the time of the struggle. Moreover we have fully remitted to all, clergy and laity, and—as far as pertains to us—have pardoned fully all the transgressions committed, on the occasion of that same struggle, from Easter of the sixteenth year of our reign until the re-establishment of peace. In witness of which, moreover, we have caused to be drawn up for them letters patent of lord Stephen, archbishop of Canterbury, lord Henry, archbishop of Dublin, and the aforesaid bishops and master Pandulf, regarding that surety and the aforesaid concessions.

63. Wherefore we will and firmly decree that the English church shall be free, and that the subjects of our realm shall have and hold all the aforesaid liberties, rights and concessions, duly and in peace, freely and quietly, fully and entirely, for themselves and their heirs, from us and our heirs, in all matters and in all places, forever, as has been said. Moreover it has been sworn, on our part as well as on the part of the barons, that all these above mentioned provisions shall be observed with good faith and without evil intent. The witnesses being the above mentioned and many others. Given through our hand, in the plain called Runnimede between Windsor and Stanes, on the fifteenth day of June, in the seventeenth year of our reign.

— 57 —

THE CHARTER OF KING PHILIP AUGUSTUS TO THE UNIVERSITY OF PARIS, 1200 [1]

The organization of medieval universities was very informal by American standards. When one of them did obtain a charter granting privileges from a king, lord, or pope, it was jealously guarded. Indeed, the book that appears on many university seals is the one in which the various privileges were preserved. This privilege is the first granted by a monarch, in this case Philip II Augustus to the University of Paris, that has survived.

✓   ✓   ✓

. . . Also, concerning the safety of the students at Paris in the future, by the advice of our subjects we have ordained as follows: we will cause all the citizens of Paris to swear that if anyone sees an injury done to any student by any layman, he will testify truthfully to this, nor will anyone withdraw in order not to see [the act]. And if it shall happen that anyone strikes a student, except in self-defense, especially if he strikes the student with a weapon, a club or a stone, all laymen who see [the act] shall in good faith seize the malefactor or malefactors and deliver them to our judge; nor shall they withdraw in order not to see the act, or seize the malefactor, or testify to the truth. Also, whether the malefactor is seized in open crime or not, we will make a legal and full examination through clerks or laymen or certain lawful persons; and our count and our judges shall do the same. . . .

Also, neither our provost nor our judges shall lay hands on a student for any offence whatever; nor shall they

[1] Univ. of Penn., "Trans. and Rep.," II, 3, pp. 4-7.

place him in our prison, unless such a crime has been
committed by the student, that he ought to be arrested.
And in that case, our judge shall arrest him on the spot,
without striking him at all, unless he resists, and shall
hand him over to the ecclesiastical judge, who ought to
guard him in order to satisfy us and the one suffering the
injury. And if a serious crime has been committed, our
judge shall go or shall send to see what is done with the
student. If, indeed, the student does not resist arrest and
yet suffers any injury, we will exact satisfaction for it,
according to the aforesaid examination and the aforesaid
oath. Also our judges shall not lay hands on the chattels
of the students at Paris for any crime whatever. But if it
shall seem that these ought to be sequestrated, they shall
be sequestrated and guarded after sequestration by the
ecclesiastical judge. . . .

Concerning the lay servants of the students who do not
owe to us *burgensiam* or *residentiam,* and do not live by
traffic, and through whom the scholars do not do any
injury to any one, it shall be as follows: neither we nor
our judge shall lay hands on them unless they commit an
open crime, for which we or our judge ought to arrest
them. In accordance, truly, with the tenor of the privilege
which we have granted to the students at Paris, we are
not willing that the canons of Paris and their servants
should be included in this privilege. . . .

In order, moreover, that these [decrees] may be kept
more carefully and may be established forever by a fixed
law, we have decided that our present provost and the
people of Paris shall affirm by an oath, in the presence
of the scholars, that they will carry out in good faith all
the above-mentioned. And always in the future, whosoever
receives from us the office of provost in Paris, among the
other initiatory acts of his office, namely, on the first or
second Sunday, in one of the churches of Paris,—after
he has been summoned for the purpose,—shall affirm by
an oath, publicly in the presence of the scholars, that he
will keep in good faith all the above-mentioned . . .

— 58 —

STUDENT LIFE AT THE UNIVERSITY OF PARIS[1]

The conduct of the students at Paris would have driven the modern dean to his grave. There were frequent rows between town and gown to be sure, but perhaps more serious were the fights between the students themselves, and especially between the different nations of students. They realized their special legal position and often were armed with clubs if not knives. Many were not students at all, but were wasting their lives in gay and violent living of which the Goliardic songs offer a glimpse. The passage following is by Jacques de Vitry (ca. 1180–ca. 1240) a prominent cleric and bishop who, among other things, preached the crusade against the Albigensians in the winter of 1211-1212.

✓   ✓   ✓

Almost all the students at Paris, foreigners and natives, did absolutely nothing except learn or hear something new. Some studied merely to acquire knowledge, which is curiosity; others to acquire fame, which is vanity; others still for the sake of gain, which is cupidity and the vice of simony. Very few studied for their own edification, or that of others. They wrangled and disputed not merely about the various sects or about some discussions; but the differences between the countries also caused dissensions, hatreds and virulent animosities among them, and they impudently uttered all kinds of affronts and insults against one another.

They affirmed that the English were drunkards and had tails; the sons of France proud, effeminate and carefully adorned like women. They said that the Germans were

[1] Univ. of Penn., "Trans. and Rep.," II, 3, pp. 9-21.

furious and obscene at their feasts; the Normans, vain
and boastful; the Poitevans, traitors and always adven-
turers. The Burgundians they considered vulgar and
stupid. The Bretons were reputed to be fickle and
changeable, and were often reproached for the death of
Arthur. The Lombards were called avaricious, vicious
and cowardly; the Romans, seditious, turbulent and slan-
derous; the Sicilians, tyrannical and cruel; the inhabitants
of Brabant, men of blood, incendiaries, brigands and
ravishers; the Flemish, fickle, prodigal, gluttonous, yield-
ing as butter, and slothful. After such insults from words
they often came to blows.

I will not speak of those logicians before whose eyes
flitted constantly "the lice of Egypt," that is to say, all
the sophistical subtleties, so that no one could compre-
hend their eloquent discourses in which, as says Isaiah,
"there is no wisdom." As to the doctors of theology,
"seated in Moses' seat," they were swollen with learning,
but their charity was not edifying. Teaching and not
practicing, they have "become as sounding brass or a
tinkling cymbal," or like a canal of stone, always dry,
which ought to carry water to "the bed of spices." They
not only hated one another, but by their flatteries they
enticed away the students of others; each one seeking his
own glory, but caring not a whit about the welfare of
souls.

— 59 —

CHARTER OF THE POPE TO THE UNIVERSITY OF PARIS, 1231[1]

The earliest, most important charter Paris received was from Pope Gregory IX and was partially the result of the students having dispersed and sworn not to reassemble. He confirms their privileges and even grants the University the right to suspend all courses, a right which was not revoked until 1499.

↗   ↗   ↗

Gregory, the bishop, servant of the servants of God, to his beloved sons, all the masters and students at Paris—greeting and apostolic benediction. . . .

. . . Concerning the condition of the students and schools, we have decided that the following should be observed: each chancellor, appointed hereafter at Paris, at the time of his installation, in the presence of the bishop, or at the command of the latter in the chapter at Paris—two masters of the students having been summoned for this purpose and present in behalf of the university—shall swear that, in good faith, according to his conscience, he will not receive as professors of theology and canon law any but suitable men, at a suitable place and time, according to the condition of the city and the honor and glory of those branches of learning; and he will reject all who are unworthy without respect to persons or nations. Before licensing anyone, during three months, dating from the time when the license is requested, the chancellor shall make diligent inquiries of all the masters of theology present in the city, and of all other honest and learned men through whom the truth can be ascertained, concerning the life, knowledge, capacity, purpose, prospects and other qualities needful in such persons; and after the inquiries, in good faith and according to his conscience, he shall grant or deny the license to the candidate, as shall seem fitting and expedient. The masters of theology and canon law, when they begin to lecture, shall take a public oath that they will give true testimony on the above points. The chancellor shall also swear, that he will in no way reveal the advice of the masters, to their injury; the liberty and privileges being maintained in their full vigor for the canons at Paris, as they were in the beginning. Moreover, the chancellor shall promise to examine in good faith the masters in medicine and arts and in the other branches, to admit only the worthy and to reject the unworthy.

In other matters, because confusion easily creeps in where there is no order, we grant to you the right of making constitutions and ordinances regulating the manner and time of lectures and disputations, the costume to be worn, the burial of the dead; and also concerning the bachelors, who are to lecture and at what hours, and on what they are to lecture; and concerning the prices of the lodgings or the interdiction of the same; and concerning a fit punishment for those who violate your constitutions or ordinances, by exclusion from your society. And if, perchance, the assessment of the lodgings is taken from you, or anything else is lacking, or an injury or outrageous damage, such as death or the mutilation of a limb, is inflicted on one of you, unless through a suitable admonition satisfaction is rendered within fifteen days, you may suspend your lectures until you have received full satisfaction. And if it happens that anyone of you is unlawfully imprisoned, unless the injury ceases on a remonstrance from you, you may, if you judge it expedient, suspend your lectures immediately.

We command, moreover, that the bishop of Paris shall so chastise the excesses of the guilty, that the honor of the student shall be preserved and evil deeds shall not remain unpunished. But in no way shall the innocent be seized on account of the guilty; nay rather, if a probable suspicion arises against any one, he shall be detained honorably and on giving suitable bail he shall be freed, without any exactions from the jailors. But if, perchance, such a crime has been committed that imprisonment is necessary, the bishop shall detain the criminal in his prison. The chancellor is forbidden to keep him in his prison. We also forbid holding a student for a debt contracted by another, since this is interdicted by canonical and legitimate sanctions. Neither the bishop nor his officials nor the chancellor shall exact a pecuniary penalty for removing an excommunication or any other censure of any kind. Nor shall the chancellor demand from the masters who are licensed an oath, or obedience, or any pledge; nor shall he receive any emolument or promise from granting a license, but be content with the abovementioned oath.

Also, the vacation in summer is not to exceed one month, and the bachelors, if they wish, can continue their lectures in vacation time. Moreover, we prohibit more expressly the students from carrying weapons in the city, and the university from protecting those who disturb the peace and study. And those who call themselves students, but do not frequent the schools, or acknowledge any master, are in no way to enjoy the liberties of the students. . . .

Truly, because the masters and students, who harassed by damages and injuries, have taken a mutual oath to depart from Paris and have broken up the school, have seemed to be waging a contest not so much for their own benefit as for the common good: we, consulting the needs and advantages of the whole church, wish and command that after the privileges have been granted to the masters and students by our most dearly beloved son in Christ, the illustrious king of the French, and amends have been paid by the malefactors, they shall study at Paris and shall not be marked by any infamy or irregularity on account of their staying away or return. . . .

— 60 —

THE RULE OF ST. FRANCIS, 1223[1]

The two mendicant orders, Dominicans and Franciscans, were in some ways a response to the heresies such as the Albigensian and Waldensian of the twelfth century. The friars (Latin frater—brother) increased very rapidly, and it is a characteristic that they were not bound to a monastery but roamed the highways and byways. It is significant that they were not subject to the authority of the bishop in whose diocese they might be, but to the pope. St. Francis did not write the Rule of his order, which also served as the model for that of the Dominicans, but it reflects his advocacy of poverty, love, and brotherhood.

✓   ✓   ✓

1. This is the rule and way of living of the minorite brothers: namely to observe the holy Gospel of our Lord Jesus Christ, living in obedience, without personal possessions, and in chastity. Brother Francis promises obedience and reverence to our lord pope Honorius, and to his successors who canonically enter upon their office, and to the Roman Church. And the other brothers shall be bound to obey brother Francis and his successors.

2. If any persons shall wish to adopt this form of living, and shall come to our brothers, they shall send them to their provincial ministers; to whom alone, and to no others, permission is given to receive brothers. But the ministers shall diligently examine them in the matter of the catholic faith and the ecclesiastical sacraments. And if they believe all these, and are willing to faithfully confess them and observe them steadfastly to the end; and if they have no wives, or if they have them and the wives

[1] Henderson, *Documents,* pp. 344-349.

have already entered a monastery, or if they shall have given them permission to do so—they themselves having already taken a vow of continence by the authority of the bishop of the diocese, and their wives being of such age that no suspicion can arise in connection with them: —the ministers shall say unto them the word of the holy Gospel, to the effect that they shall go and sell all that they have and strive to give it to the poor. But if they shall not be able to do this, their good will is enough. And the brothers and their ministers shall be on their guard and not concern themselves for their temporal goods; so that they may freely do with those goods exactly as God inspires them. But if advice is required, the ministers shall have permission to send them to some God-fearing men by whose counsel they shall dispense their goods to the poor. Afterwards there shall be granted to them the garments of probation: namely two gowns without cowls and a belt, and hose and a cape down to the belt; unless to these same ministers something else may at some time seem to be preferable in the sight of God. But, when the year of probation is over, they shall be received into obedience; promising always to observe that manner of living, and this Rule. And, according to the mandate of the lord pope, they shall never be allowed to break these bonds. For according to the holy Gospel, no one putting his hand to the plough and looking back is fit for the kingdom of God. And those who have now promised obedience shall have one gown with a cowl, and another, if they wish it, without a cowl. And those who are compelled by necessity, may wear shoes. And all the brothers shall wear humble garments, and may repair them with sack cloth and other remnants, with the benediction of God. And I warn and exhort them lest they despise or judge men whom they shall see clad in soft garments and in colors, using delicate food and drink; but each one shall the rather judge and despise himself.

3. The clerical brothers shall perform the divine service according to the order of the holy Roman Church; excepting the psalter, of which they may have extracts. But the lay brothers shall say twenty-four Paternosters at matins, five at the service of praise, seven each at the first, third, sixth and ninth hour, twelve at vespers, seven

at the completorium; and they shall pray for the dead. And they shall fast from the feast of All Saints to the Nativity of the Lord; but as to the holy season of Lent, which begins from the Epiphany of the Lord and continues forty days, which the Lord consecrated with his holy fast—those who fast during it shall be blessed of the Lord, and those who do not wish to fast shall not be bound to do so; but otherwise they shall fast until the Resurrection of the Lord. But at other times the brothers shall not be bound to fast save on the sixth day (Friday); but in time of manifest necessity the brothers shall not be bound to fast with their bodies. But I advise, warn and exhort my brothers in the Lord Jesus Christ, that, when they go into the world, they shall not quarrel, nor contend with words, nor judge others. But they shall be gentle, peaceable and modest, merciful and humble, honestly speaking with all, as is becoming. And they ought not to ride unless they are compelled by manifest necessity or by infirmity. Into whatever house they enter they shall first say: peace be to this house. And according to the holy Gospel it is lawful for them to eat of all the dishes which are placed before them.

4. I firmly command all the brothers by no means to receive coin or money, of themselves or through an intervening person. But for the needs of the sick and for clothing the other brothers, the ministers alone and the guardians shall provide through spiritual friends, as it may seem to them that necessity demands, according to time, place and cold temperature. This one thing being always regarded, that, as has been said, they receive neither coin nor money.

5. Those brothers to whom God has given the ability to labor, shall labor faithfully and devoutly; in such way that idleness, the enemy of the soul, being excluded, they may not extinguish the spirit of holy prayer and devotion; to which other temporal things should be subservient. As a reward, moreover, for their labor, they may receive for themselves and their brothers the necessaries of life, but not coin or money; and this humbly, as becomes the servants of God and the followers of most holy poverty.

6. The brothers shall appropriate nothing to themselves, neither a house, nor a place, nor anything; but as

pilgrims and strangers in this world, in poverty and humility serving God, they shall confidently go seeking for alms. Nor need they be ashamed, for the Lord made Himself poor for us in this world. This is that height of most lofty poverty, which has constituted you my most beloved brothers heirs and kings of the kingdom of Heaven, has made you poor in possessions, has exalted you in virtues. This be your portion, which leads on to the land of the living. Adhering to it absolutely, most beloved brothers, you will wish to have for ever in Heaven nothing else than the name of our Lord Jesus Christ. . . .

7. But if any of the brothers at the instigation of the enemy shall mortally sin: for those sins concerning which it has been ordained among the brothers that recourse must be had to the provincial ministers, the aforesaid brothers shall be bound to have recourse to them, as quickly as they can, without delay. But those ministers, if they are priests, shall with mercy enjoin penance upon them. But if they are not priests, they shall cause it to be enjoined upon them through others, priests of the order; according as it seems to them to be most expedient in the sight of God. And they ought to be on their guard lest they grow angry and be disturbed on account of the sin of any one; for wrath and indignation impede love in themselves and in others.

8. All the brothers shall be bound always to have one of the brothers of that order as general minister and servant of the whole fraternity, and shall be firmly bound to obey him. When he dies, the election of a successor shall be made by the provincial ministers and guardians, in the chapter held at Pentecost; in which the provincial ministers are bound always to come together in whatever place shall be designated by the general minister. And this, once in three years; or at another greater or lesser interval, according as shall be ordained by the aforesaid minister. And if, at any time, it shall be apparent to the whole body of the provincial ministers and guardians that the aforesaid minister does not suffice for the service and common utility of the brothers: the aforesaid brothers to whom the right of election has been given shall be

bound, in the name of God, to elect another as their guardian. But after the chapter held at Pentecost the ministers and guardians can, if they wish it and it seems expedient for them, in that same year call together, once, their brothers, in their districts, to a chapter.

9. The brothers may not preach in the bishopric of any bishop if they have been forbidden to by him. And no one of the brothers shall dare to preach at all to the people, unless he have been examined and approved by the general minister of this fraternity, and the office of preacher have been conceded to him. I also exhort those same brothers that, in the preaching which they do, their expressions shall be chaste and chosen, to the utility and edification of the people; announcing to them vices and virtues, punishment and glory, with briefness of discourse; for the words were brief which the Lord spoke upon earth.

10. The brothers who are the ministers and servants of the other brothers shall visit and admonish their brothers and humbly and lovingly correct them; not teaching them anything which is against their soul and against our Rule. But the brothers who are subjected to them shall remember that, before God, they have discarded their own wills. Wherefore I firmly command them that they obey their ministers in all things which they have promised God to observe, and which are not contrary to their souls and to our Rule. And wherever there are brothers who know and recognize that they can not spiritually observe the Rule, they may and should have recourse to their ministers. But the ministers shall receive them lovingly and kindly, and shall exercise such familiarity towards them, that they may speak and act towards them as masters to their servants; for so it ought to be, that the ministers should be the servants of all the brothers. I warn and exhort, moreover, in Christ Jesus the Lord, that the brothers be on their guard against all pride, vainglory, envy, avarice, care and anxiety for this world, detraction and murmuring. And they shall not take trouble to teach those ignorant of letters, but shall pay heed to this that they desire to have the spirit of God and its holy workings; that they pray always to God with a pure

heart; that they have humility, patience, in persecution and infirmity; and that they love those who persecute, revile and attack us. . . .

11. I firmly command all the brothers not to have suspicious intercourse or to take counsel with women. And, with the exception of those to whom special permission has been given by the Apostolic Chair, let them not enter nunneries. Neither may they become fellow godparents with men or women, lest from this cause a scandal may arise among the brothers or concerning brothers.

12. Whoever of the brothers by divine inspiration may wish to go among the Saracens and other infidels, shall seek permission to do so from their provincial ministers. But to none shall the ministers give permission to go, save to those whom they shall see to be fit for the mission.

Furthermore, through their obedience I enjoin on the ministers that they demand from the lord pope one of the cardinals of the holy Roman Church, who shall be the governor, corrector and protector of that fraternity, so that, always subjected and lying at the feet of that same holy Church, steadfast in the catholic faith, we may observe poverty and humility, and the holy Gospel of our Lord Jesus Christ; as we have firmly promised.

— 61 —

THE STATUTE IN FAVOR OF THE PRINCES, 1231-1232[1]

The emperor Frederick II was primarily interested in his Sicilian and Italian possessions. He had his young son crowned King Henry VII of Germany, and the nobles

[1] O. J. Thatcher and E. H. McNeal, *A Source Book for Medieval History* (Charles Scribner's Sons, New York, 1905), pp. 238-240. Reprinted by permission of the publisher.

had slight trouble in extracting regalian powers from him. The emperor confirmed these grants to the German nobles by this statute. The effect was to free Frederick II of concern for Germany, because the aristocracy were quite content with their new powers. Frederick had already diminished the crown rights when he granted many privileges to the ecclesiastical princes in 1220.

✓ ✓ ✓

In the name of the holy and undivided Trinity. Frederick II, by divine mercy emperor of the Romans, Augustus, king of Jerusalem, king of Sicily. . . .

1. No new castles or cities shall be erected by us or by anyone else to the prejudice of the princes.

2. New markets shall not be allowed to interfere with the interests of former ones.

3. No one shall be compelled to attend any market against his will.

4. Travellers shall not be compelled to leave the old highways, unless they desire to do so.

5. We will not exercise jurisdiction within the banmile of our cities.

6. Each prince shall possess and exercise in peace according to the customs of the land the liberties, jurisdiction, and authority over counties and hundreds which are in his own possession or are held as fiefs from him.

7. Centgrafs shall receive their office from the prince or from the person who holds the land as a fief.

8. The location of the hundred court shall not be changed without the consent of the lord.

9. No nobleman shall be amenable to the hundred court.

10. The citizens who are known as *phalburgii* (*i.e.*, persons or corporations existing outside the city, but possessing political rights within it) shall be expelled from the cities.

11. Payments of wine, money, grain, and other rents, which free peasants have formerly agreed to pay (to the emperor), are hereby remitted, and shall not be collected henceforth.

12. The serfs of princes, nobles, ministerials, and churches shall not be admitted to our cities.

13. Lands and fiefs of princes, nobles, ministerials, and churches, which have been seized by our cities, shall be restored and shall never again be taken.

14. The right of the princes to furnish safe-conduct within the lands which they hold as fiefs from us shall not be infringed by us or by anyone else.

15. Inhabitants of our cities shall not be compelled by our judges to restore any possessions which they may have received from others before they moved there.

16. Notorious, condemned, and proscribed persons shall not be admitted to our cities; if they have been, they shall be driven out.

17. We will never cause any money to be coined in the land of any of the princes which shall be injurious to his coinage.

18. The jurisdiction of our cities shall not extend beyond their boundaries, unless we possess special jurisdiction in the region.

19. In our cities the plaintiff shall bring suit in the court of the accused.

20. Lands or property which are held as fiefs shall not be pawned without the consent of the lord from whom they are held.

21. No one shall be compelled to aid in the fortifying of cities unless he is legally bound to render that service.

22. Inhabitants of our cities who hold lands outside shall pay to their lords or advocates the regular dues and services, and they shall not be burdened with unjust exactions.

23. If serfs, freemen subject to advocates, or vassals of any lord, shall dwell within any of our cities, they shall not be prevented by our officials from going to their lords.

— 62 —

THE EXCOMMUNICATION OF FREDERICK II AT THE COUNCIL OF LYONS, 1245[1]

Pope Innocent IV had been friendly to the emperor before he was elected pope. Thereafter he turned on the amazing Frederick and excommunicated him. This was nothing new to the emperor, but it was the last such sentence against him, since he died in 1250.

✓   ✓   ✓

[Innocent recapitulates the efforts of the popes to maintain peace between the church and the empire and dwells upon the sins of the emperor. Then, after charging him with the particular crimes of perjury, sacrilege, heresy, and tyranny, he proceeds as follows:] We, therefore, on account of his aforesaid crimes and of his many other nefarious misdeeds, after careful deliberation with our brethren and with the holy council, acting however unworthily as the vicar of Jesus Christ on earth and knowing how it was said to us in the person of the blessed apostle Peter, *Whatsoever ye shall bind on earth shall be bound in heaven;* we announce and declare the said prince to be bound because of his sins and rejected by the Lord and deprived of all honor and dignity, and moreover by this sentence we hereby deprive him of the same since he has rendered himself so unworthy of ruling his kingdom and so unworthy of all honors and dignity; for, indeed, on account of his iniquities he has been rejected of God that he might not reign or exercise authority. All who have taken the oath of fidelity to him we absolve forever from such oath by our apostolic authority, abso-

[1] Univ. of Penn., "Trans. and Rep.," IV, 4, p. 25.

lutely forbidding anyone hereafter to obey him or look upon him as emperor or king. Let those whose duty it is to select a new emperor proceed freely with the election. But it shall be our care to provide as shall seem fitting to us for the kingdom of Sicily with the council of our brothers, the cardinals.

— 63 —

AN ALLIANCE OF GERMAN TOWNS TO PROTECT THEIR MERCHANTS, 1253[1]

This document describes a federation of Westphalian towns. It reveals the perils and inconveniences to which their merchants were exposed. Such associations were quite common and they even obtained privileges from monarchs. The most successful was among certain north German towns that came to be known as the Hanseatic League.

✦ ✦ ✦

In the name of the holy and indivisible Trinity, Amen. The magistrates, consuls, and the whole community of burghers and citizens in Münster, Dortmund, Soest, and Lippstadt, to all who may read this document, greeting:
We hereby make known to all men, now and in the future, that because of the manifold dangers to which we are constantly exposed, of capture, robbery, and many other injuries, we have, by common counsel and consent, decided to unite in a perpetual confederation under the

---

[1] James Harvey Robinson, *Readings in European History* (2 vols., Ginn and Co., New York, 1904), I, 413.

following terms, and we have mutually given and received word and oath:

First, that if any man shall take captive one of our citizens or seize his goods without just cause, we will altogether deny to him opportunity to trade in all our cities aforesaid. And if the castellan of any lord shall be the author of an injury that has been done, the afore-mentioned privileges shall be altogether withheld from the lord of that castellan, and from all his soldiers and servants, and all others dwelling with him in his cas-tle. . . .

If any robber has taken goods from one of our citizens . . . and the injured man shall go to any one of our [federated] cities seeking counsel and aid, in order that justice may be done upon the malefactor, the citizens of that city shall act as they would be obliged to act if executing justice for a similar crime committed against one of their own fellow-citizens.

And if any of our burgesses shall chance to go to any of our cities and fear to go forth because of peril to life and property, the burgesses of that city shall conduct him to a place whence his fellow-citizens can receive him in safety.

If a knight shall be denounced to us on reasonable grounds as a violator of faith and honor, we will denounce him in all our cities, and will by mutual consent withhold from him all privileges in our cities until he shall pay the whole debt for which he broke his word.

If any one of us shall buy goods taken from any of our confederates by theft or robbery . . . he shall not offer the goods at retail anywhere and shall be held guilty with the thief and robber.

— 64 —

ORDINANCE OF LOUIS IX, 1254[1]

Louis IX, or St. Louis, was in many ways the epitome of what a medieval king should be. He was devoutly religious and went on two crusades, but his greatest fame is due to his sense of justice. Although he was dominated by his mother, he had a keen sense of his royal position and supported Henry III of England and the emperor Frederick II against attempts to limit their power. He firmly and consistently enlarged and improved the administration that he had inherited from Philip II, but he did it in such a way that it added to, rather than detracted from, his prestige. The following extracts are taken from the biography of Louis that was written by his friend and companion, the lord of Joinville.

✦   ✦   ✦

We Louis, by the grace of God, king of France, order that all bailiffs, provosts, mayors, judges, receivers, and others in whatever office they may be, do each henceforth make oath that, during the time he shall hold such office, he will do strict justice to everyone, without exception of person, as well to the poor as to the rich, to the stranger as well as to the resident, and will follow such laws and customs as have been found good and approved of. Should anyone act contrary to his oath, we will and expressly command that he be punished in body and estate, according to the exigency of the case. We reserve to ourselves, and to our own discretion, the punishments that may be due to our bailiffs, judges, and other officers, and also to those employed under them.

Our treasurers, receivers, provosts, auditors of accounts, and other officers concerned in our finances, will

[1] *Chronicles of the Crusades, etc.* (Bohn ed., London, 1848), pp. 520-522.

swear that they will well and loyally guard our rents and domains, with all our rights, liberties, and privileges, without suffering them in any way to be infringed upon or abridged.

They will not themselves accept of any gift or present . . . nor consent to any presents being made to their wives or children, in order to gain their favor. . . . In like manner, they will not make any presents to any persons their superiors, to gain their favor and support. They will also swear, that whenever they shall discover any officers, sergeants, or others, who are robbers, and abuse their offices, for which they ought to be dismissed from them, and our service, they will not conceal or disguise their guilt for any gift, favor, promise, or otherwise. . . .

We likewise forbid and prohibit all our said bailiffs, provosts, mayors, judges, and others our officers, either to swear by or blaspheme the name of God, his holy mother, or the blessed saints in paradise, or to game with dice, or to frequent taverns, or houses of ill-fame, under penalty of deprivation of office and undergoing such other punishment as their crimes may deserve. . . .

We also forbid and prohibit any of our bailiffs, provosts, mayors, or others our officers, to have the boldness to acquire or purchase, by themselves or others, any lands or possessions in the districts over which they have been appointed to administer justice, without our being previously made acquainted therewith, and our leave and license first had and obtained. Should they act otherwise, we will and declare that such lands and possessions, so acquired, be confiscated to our benefit.

In like manner, we forbid any of our aforesaid superior officers, so long as they shall be in our service, to marry their sons, daughters, or other relations they may have, to any persons within their bailiwicks or district, without our special permission first obtained. We also include within the above prohibitions of acquisitions of property and marriage, all other inferior judges, or other subalterns of offices.

We likewise forbid any bailiff, provost, or other, to have too great a number of sergeants or beadles, so that the people may be aggrieved thereat.

We also forbid any of our subjects to be personally arrested or imprisoned for any debt of theirs, but what may be owed to the crown, and that any fine be levied on any of our subjects for debt.

We likewise ordain that those who may hold our provostships, viscountships, or other offices, do not sell nor transfer them to any other person without our consent. . . .

We forbid, likewise, any disseizure of possession without assigning a proper reason for it, or having our special commands to that purpose. We order that there be no additional taxes raised, nor any other imposts or customs whatever.

We will that our bailiffs, provosts, mayors, viscounts, and other our officers, who shall at any time be deprived of their offices, and dismissed our service, do remain after such dismission forty days within the districts where their appointments lay, either personally, or by sufficient proxy, to answer to those who shall be their successors, to such questions as they shall ask touching their evil deeds and the complaints made against them.

— 65 —

TAXES OF THE KINGDOM OF JERUSALEM[1]

The following list of taxes gives some idea of the commerce in the eastern Mediterranean. The letters B. and K. stand for the coins called besant and karouble.

1. The old duties command that one should take at the custom house for the sale of silk for every hundred B., 8 B. and 19 K., as duty.

[1] Univ. of Penn., "Trans. and Rep.," III, 2, pp. 19-23.

2. For the duties on cotton the rule commands that one should take per hundred, 10 B. and 18 K. as duties.

3. For the duties of pepper the rule commands that one should take per hundred 11 B. and 5 K. as duties.

4. For cinnamon the rule commands that one should take per hundred 10 B. and 18 K. as duty.

5. For wool the rule commands that one should take per hundred B., 11 B. and 10 K. as taxes.

6. For the duties of alum the rule commands that one should take per hundred, 11 B. and 5 K. as duties.

[Duty is stipulated for varnish, nutmegs and nutmeg leaves, flax, cloves and leaves of cloves, and Indian hens.]

12. For the wares which are brought by sea from the coast of Syria and which cannot be sold the rule is that they can be withdrawn and taken out of the country, but if the merchandise which cannot be sold be taken out beyond the chain they must be paid per hundred for as much as may then be in the country 8 B. per hundred, and for that which may have been sold duty must be paid to the custom house according that which is established for each kind and which one would have to pay. And be it understood that these duties shall be paid by the Saracens and by all the Syrians who may come with wares into this kingdom.

13. For the duties on musc the rule commands that one should take per hundred B., 8 B. and 1/3 as duty.

14. For the duty upon aloe wood the rule commands that one should take 9 B. and 1/3 per hundred as duty.

15. For the duties on sugar for that which is imported and exported by land and by sea, the rule commands that one should take per hundred, 5 B. as duty.

16. For the duties per camel's load of sugar the rule commands that one should take 4 B. as duty.

17. For the duty on sugar which is brought by beasts of burden the rule commands that one should take 1 raboin per load as duty.

18. For all things which are exported by land to be taken to the Paynims the rule commands that one should take as duty per Besant 1 K.

[Duty is stipulated for flax intransit imported from Babylon to Damascus, salt fish imported from Babylon, alcana, all the spices of retail shop-keepers, sesamum, oil of sesamum, incense, cardemoine, ivory, sarcocoll, galega, twigs and leaves of lavender, myrodolan, cinnamon, rhubarb, ginger, camphor, borage, aspic, gariophylus; an internal tax is fixed for ammonia, Nabeth sugar, dates; duty on emery (Saracen and Syrian licorice pays a higher duty than French licorice) sulfur of arsenic, camphor root; straps and saddles exported from Jerusalem; an internal tax on yellow sulfur of arsenic; duty on libanotis.]

49. It is understood that the rule commands that one should take on all planks and beams which are exported by land, as duty the quarter of what they cost.

50. It is understood that the rule commands that one should take as duty on planks used to construct threshing floors the tenth of what they cost.

51. It is understood that the rule commands that one should take upon salt fish exported from the city the quarter of what it cost as duty.

[Duty or an internal tax or both are stipulated for fruit, hens, rafters, olives, wine, Damascus thread, senna, red currants, shoes bought by Saracens, wheat, eggs, hens and pullets, imported goats, geese, oil, nut gall, imported wool, wax and pens.]

— 66 —

THE STATUTE OF MORTMAIN, 1279[1]

The purpose of this act of Edward I of England was to prevent lords from fraudulently granting land to the church in order to escape their feudal obligations. The

[1] Stubbs, *Charters*, pp. 458-459.

church was often successful in evading feudal dues to the detriment of the sovereign, and so it is to receive land only with his permission.

✓   ✓   ✓

The king to his justices of the bench, greeting. Whereas formerly it was provided that men of religion should not enter into the fiefs of anyone without the approval and license of the chief lords of whom these fiefs are held immediately; and afterwards men of religion nevertheless have entered into their own fiefs as well as into those of others, by appropriating them, purchasing them, and sometimes receiving them as the gift of others, whereby the services which are owed of such fiefs, and which originally were provided for the defense of the realm are withdrawn without just cause, and the chief lords thereafter lose their escheats; we, for the benefit of the kingdom and wishing to provide a suitable remedy, on the counsel of our prelates, counts and other faithful of our realm who are of our council, have provided, established, and ordained, that no man of religion or any other whosoever, shall presume to buy or sell any lands or tenements, or in the form of a gift, rent, or any other title whatever to receive them from anyone, or to appropriate to himself any place whatever in any other way, by art or by wile, whereby such lands and tenements may come into mortmain; under pain of forfeiting them. We have provided further that if anyone, religious or other, presumes in any way either by art or wile to violate the present statute, it shall be lawful for us and other immediate lords-in-chief of the fief so alienated, to enter it within a year from the time of such alienation and to hold it in fee and in inheritance. And if the immediate lord-in-chief is negligent and unwilling to enter into that fief within a year, then it shall be lawful for the next mediate lord-in-chief of that fief within the ensuing half year to enter that fief and to hold it, as indicated; and each mediate lord may do this if the nearer lord be lax in entering such a fief as has been related. And if all such chief lords of such a fief, who shall be of full age and within the four seas and out of prison, shall be negligent or remiss in this matter for one year, immediately after the year is completed from the time when such purchases, gifts, or other appropriations have been made, we shall seize such lands and tenements into our possession, and thence shall enfeoff others for certain services to be done to us for the defence of our kingdom; saving to the chief lords of the these fiefs their wardships, escheats and other things pertaining to them, and the services due and accustomed from them. And therefore we command you to have the aforesaid statute read in your presence and henceforth strictly kept and observed. By witness of the king at Westminster, the 15th day of November, the 7th year of our reign.

— 67 —

THE STATUTE OF *QUIA EMPTORES*, 1290[1]

This statute of Edward I does not prevent subinfeuda-tion but it does make it unattractive, because the newly created vassal would become the vassal of the feoffor's lord. The feoffor would then have deprived himself of services which had previously been rendered by the holder of that land. The superior lords, especially the monarch, will gain in the long run by acquiring more vassals.

✓   ✓   ✓

Since the purchasers of lands and tenements from the fiefs of magnates and others have often in the past entered their fiefs to the prejudice of the lords, because the freeholders of these magnates and others have sold their lands and tenements to them to be held in fee by

[1] Stubbs, *Charters,* pp. 478-479.

themselves and their heirs of their feoffors and not of
the chief lords of the fiefs, whereby the same chief lords
have often lost the escheats, marriages, and wardships
of the lands and tenements pertaining to their fiefs, which
has seemed very hard and difficult to those magnates and
other lords, and in this case evident disinheritance; the
lord king in his parliament at Westminster after Easter
in the eighteenth year of his reign, in the fortnight of
St. John the Baptist, at the instance of the magnates of
his realm, granted, provided and decreed that henceforth
it shall be lawful for any free man to sell his land or
tenement or a part of it as he pleases; in such manner,
nevertheless, that the feofee shall hold that land or tenement from the same chief lord and by the same service
and customs by which his feoffor previously held it. And
if he should sell any part of his lands or tenements to
anyone, the feoffee shall hold it immediately of the chief
lord, and shall immediately be burdened with the amount
of service that belongs or ought to belong to that lord for
that parcel, according to the amount of land or tenement
sold; and, thus, there will drop off from the chief lord
that part of the service owed by the hand of the feoffor,
for thence the feoffee owes to the same chief lord, according to the amount of land or tenement sold; for that
portion of services thus owed he is answerable and responsible. And let it be known that, through the aforesaid
sales or purchases of lands or tenements, or any part of
them, in no way are those lands or tenements in part or in
whole, to come into mortmain, by art or craft, contrary to
the form of the statute recently issued on this, etc.

And let it be known that that statute concerning lands
sold applies only to those holding in fee simple, etc.; and
that it extends to future time; and it shall begin to take
effect at the next feast of St. Andrew, etc.

— 68 —

CONFIRMATION OF THE CHARTERS, 1297[1]

Magna Carta and the Charter of the Forest are here confirmed and King Edward I agrees that he will levy no extraordinary tax without the common assent of the kingdom. Since this could be only obtained in parliament, it had gained an important measure of control in the matter of taxation. Edward's military campaigns in Wales and Scotland had been very expensive, his decision to fight in Flanders against France annoyed the barons, while the clergy were aroused by his seizures of their land following the bull of Boniface VIII, Clericis laicos. This charter appeased the dissidents.

↗   ↗   ↗

I. Edward, by the grace of God, king of England, lord of Ireland, and duke of Aquitaine, to all who shall see or hear these present letters, greeting. Know that, for the honor of God and the holy church and the benefit of all our kingdom, we have granted for ourselves and our heirs that the great charter of liberties and the charter of the forest which were made by the common assent of the whole realm in the time of King Henry, our father, are to be maintained in all their points without any weakening. And we will that these same charters be sent under our seal to our justices, those of the forest as well as the others, to all the sheriffs of the counties and to all our other ministers, to all our cities throughout the land, together with our writs, which will provide that the aforesaid charters are to be published, and that they are to tell the people that we have confirmed them to be upheld in all their points; and to our justices, sheriffs, mayors and

[1] Stubbs, *Charters,* pp. 494-496.

other ministers whose duty it is to administer the law of the land under us and by our guidance, shall allow the same charters in all their points in pleas or in judgments before them; that is to say the great charter of liberties as common law and the charter of the forest according to the assizes of the forest, for the improvement of our people.

II. And we will that if any judgment is given henceforth contrary to the points of the aforesaid charters by the justices and by our other ministers who hold pleas before themselves contrary to the provisions of the charters, it will be defaulted and held for nothing.

III. And we will that these same charters with this our seal shall be sent to cathedral churches throughout our realm, and shall stay there; and that they shall be read twice a year before the people.

IV. And that archbishops and bishops shall pronounce sentences of great excommunication against all those who shall violate the aforesaid charters by deed or word or counsel, or on any point break or undo them. And these sentences will be pronounced and published twice a year by the aforesaid prelates. And if these prelates, bishops or any of them are negligent in making the aforesaid denunciation, they will be reproved and ordered to make this same denunciation in the aforesaid form by the archbishops of Canterbury and York who are in office at the time as is fitting.

V. And because some people in our realm fear that the aids and *mises* which they have previously paid for our wars and other needs by their liberality and good will, in whatever manner they were paid, can become a servile dues for them and their heirs, because they may be found again on the rolls; and also the prises that have been taken in our name throughout the kingdom by our ministers: we have granted for us and for our heirs that we will not make customary any aids, *mises,* or prises on account of anything that has been done or that is on the rolls or that can be found in any way.

VI. And we have also granted for us and for our heirs to the archbishops, bishops, abbots and priors and to the other people of the holy church, and to the earls and barons and to all the community of the land, that on no account will we take this manner of aids, *mises,* and prises from our realm except by the common assent of all the realm, and for the common benefit of the same realm, saving the ancient aids and prises due and accustomed.

VII. And because most of the community of the kingdom feel themselves hard oppressed by the maltote on wools, that is to say from each sack of wool 40 shillings, and have prayed us to release them, we have, at their prayer, fully released them; and we have granted that we and our heirs will not take this nor another without their common assent and their good will; saving to us and to our heirs the custom on woolens, skins and leather that had been previously granted by the community of the aforesaid realm. . . .

— 69 —

THE BULL *CLERICIS LAICOS,* 1296[1]

For several centuries princes had received money from the clergy under various arrangements and compromises; during the Crusades they had combined their resources. But by the end of the thirteenth century the kings of England and France were more hard pressed for funds than ever, and in 1295 Edward I and Philip IV asked for contributions from their clergy for the war they planned in Gascony. Pope Boniface VIII, a fiery and ambitious old Italian noble, forbade the clergy to give such funds by this bull which states the issue but makes no new papal claims. The reaction of both kings was immediate: Edward placed his clergy outside the law, Philip refused to allow any money to leave France for Rome. The pope thereupon retreated and in August, 1297, revoked the bull.

[1] Henderson, *Documents,* pp. 432-434.

Bishop Boniface, servant of the servants of God, in perpetual memory of this matter. Antiquity teaches us that laymen are in a high degree hostile to the clergy, a fact which also the experiences of the present times declare and make manifest; inasmuch as, not content within their own bounds, they strive after what is forbidden, and loose the reins in pursuit of what is unlawful. Nor have they the prudence to consider that all jurisdiction is denied them over the clergy—over both the persons and the goods of ecclesiastics. On the prelates of the churches and on ecclesiastical persons, monastic and secular, they impose heavy burdens, tax them and declare levies upon them. They exact and extort from them the half, the tenth or twentieth or some other portion or quota of their revenues or of their goods; and they attempt in many ways to subject them to slavery and reduce them to their sway. And, with grief do we mention it, some prelates of the churches and ecclesiastical persons, fearing where they ought not to fear, seeking a transitory peace, dreading more to offend the temporal than the eternal majesty, without obtaining the authority or permission of the apostolic chair, do acquiesce, not so much rashly, as improvidently, in the abuses of such persons. We, therefore, wishing to put a stop to such iniquitous acts, by the counsel of our brothers, of the apostolic authority, have decreed: that whatever prelates, or ecclesiastical persons, monastic or secular, of whatever grade, condition or standing, shall pay, or promise, or agree to pay as levies or talliages to laymen the tenth, twentieth or hundredth part of their own and their churches' revenues or goods—or any other quantity, portion or quota of those same revenues or goods, of their estimated or of their real value—under the name of an aid, loan, subvention, subsidy or gift, or under any other name, manner or clever pretence, without the authority of that same chair: likewise emperors, kings, or princes, dukes, counts or barons, podestas, captains or officials or rectors—by whatever name they are called, whether of cities, castles, or any places whatever, wherever situated; and any other persons, of whatever pre-eminence, condition or standing who shall impose, exact or receive such payments, or shall anywhere arrest, seize or presume to take possession of the belongings of churches or ecclesiastical persons which are deposited in the sacred buildings, or shall order them to be arrested, seized or taken possession of, or shall receive them when taken possession of, seized or arrested—also all who shall knowingly give aid, counsel or favour in the aforesaid things, whether publicly or secretly :—shall incur, by the act itself, the sentence of excommunication. Corporations, moreover, which shall be guilty in these matters, we place under the ecclesiastical interdict. The prelates and above-mentioned ecclesiastical persons we strictly command, by virtue of their obedience and under penalty of deposition, that they by no means acquiesce in such demands, without express permission of the aforesaid chair; and that they pay nothing under pretext of any obligation, promise and confession made hitherto, or to be made hereafter before such constitution, notice or decree shall come to their notice; nor shall the aforesaid secular persons in any way receive anything. And if they shall pay, or if the aforesaid persons shall receive, they shall fall by the act itself under sentence of excommunication. From the aforesaid sentences of excommunication and interdict, moreover, no one shall be able to be absolved, except in the throes of death, without the authority and special permission of the apostolic chair; since it is our intention by no means to pass over with dissimulation so horrid an abuse of the secular powers. Notwithstanding any privileges whatever—under whatever tenor, form, or manner or conception of words—that have been granted to emperors, kings, and other persons mentioned above; as to which privileges we will that, against what we have here laid down, they in no wise avail any person or persons. Let no man at all, then, infringe this page of our constitution, prohibition or decree, or, with rash daring, act counter to it; but if any one shall presume to attempt this, he shall know that he is about to incur the indignation of Almighty God and of His blessed apostles Peter and Paul.

Given at Rome at St. Peter's on the sixth day before the Calends of March (Feb. 25), in the second year of our pontificate.

— 70 —

THE BULL *UNAM SANCTAM*, 1302[1]

Although the controversy over the taxation of the
clergy by laymen was resolved, Philip IV continued to
resist certain claims of Boniface VIII. The issue was thus
changed to the larger one of papal supremacy. Charges
and claims were made in Rome and Paris, but the matter
was brought to a head when Philip accused Bishop Ber-
nard Saiset of Pamiers of treasonable actions. The pope
claimed he should be tried in his court, Philip said that it
was a case for his court. Boniface stated his position in
the bull that follows. It will be noticed that once again
his claims are hardly new, but they are made with un-
usual force and precision. This time neither side retreated,
and the upshot was the manhandling of Boniface by
Philip's minister William de Nogaret at Anagni in Sep-
tember 1303. Boniface died a month later, his successor
lived only a year, and when the archbishop of Bordeaux
was elected pope as Clement V, he settled in Avignon,
where his successors were to reside for seventy years.
The medieval papacy was no more.

✔   ✔   ✔

We are compelled, our faith urging us, to believe and
to hold—and we do firmly believe and simply confess—
that there is one holy catholic and apostolic church, outside of which there is neither salvation nor remission of
sins; her Spouse proclaiming it in the canticles: "My
dove, my undefiled is but one, she is the choice one of her
that bare her"; which represents one mystic body, of
which body the head is Christ; but of Christ, God. In
this church there is one Lord, one faith and one baptism.
There was one ark of Noah, indeed, at the time of the

[1] Henderson, *Documents*, pp. 435-437.

flood, symbolizing one church; and this being finished in one cubit had, namely, one Noah as helmsman and commander. And, with the exception of this ark, all things existing upon the earth were, as we read, destroyed. This church, moreover, we venerate as the only one, the Lord saying through His prophet: "Deliver my soul from the sword, my darling from the power of the dog." He prayed at the same time for His soul—that is, for Himself the Head—and for His body—which body, namely, he called the one and only church on account of the unity of the faith promised, of the sacraments, and of the love of the church. She is that seamless garment of the Lord which was not cut but which fell by lot. Therefore of this one and only church there is one body and one head— not two heads as if it were a monster:—Christ, namely, and the vicar of Christ, St. Peter, and the successor of Peter. For the Lord Himself said to Peter, Feed my sheep. My sheep, He said, using a general term, and not designating these or those particular sheep; from which it is plain that He committed to Him *all* His sheep. If, then, the Greeks or others say that they were not committed to the care of Peter and his successors, they necessarily confess that they are not of the sheep of Christ; for the Lord says, in John, that there is one fold, one shepherd and one only. We are told by the word of the gospel that in this His fold there are two swords,—a spiritual, namely, and a temporal. For when the apostles said "Behold here are two swords"—when, namely, the apostles were speaking in the church—the Lord did not reply that this was too much, but enough. Surely he who denies that the temporal sword is in the power of Peter wrongly interprets the word of the Lord when He says: "Put up thy sword in its scabbard." Both swords, the spiritual and the material, therefore, are in the power of the church; the one, indeed, to be wielded for the church, the other by the church; the one by the hand of the priest, the other by the hand of kings and knights, but at the will and sufferance of the priest. One sword, moreover, ought to be under the other, and the temporal authority to be subjected to the spiritual. For when the apostle says "there is no power but of God, and the powers that are of God are ordained," they would not be ordained unless sword were under sword and the lesser one, as it were, were led by the other to great deeds. For according to St. Dionysius the law of divinity is to lead the lowest through the intermediate to the highest things. Not therefore, according to the law of the universe, are all things reduced to order equally and immediately; but the lowest through the intermediate, the intermediate through the higher. But that the spiritual exceeds any earthly power in dignity and nobility we ought the more openly to confess the more spiritual things excel temporal ones. This also is made plain to our eyes from the giving of tithes, and the benediction and the sanctification; from the acceptation of this same power, from the control over those same things. For, the truth bearing witness, the spiritual power has to establish the earthly power, and to judge it if it be not good. Thus concerning the church and the ecclesiastical power is verified the prophecy of Jeremiah: "See, I have this day set thee over the nations and over the kingdoms," and the other things which follow. Therefore if the earthly power err it shall be judged by the spiritual power; but if the lesser spiritual power err, by the greater. But if the greatest, it can be judged by God alone, not by man, the apostle bearing witness. A spiritual man judges all things, but he himself is judged by no one. This authority, moreover, even though it is given to man and exercised through man, is not human but rather divine, being given by divine lips to Peter and founded on a rock for him and his successors through Christ himself whom he has confessed; the Lord himself saying to Peter: "Whatsoever thou shalt bind," etc. Whoever, therefore, resists this power thus ordained by God, resists the ordination of God, unless he makes believe, like the Manichean, that there are two beginnings. This we consider false and heretical, since by the testimony of Moses, not "in the beginnings," but "in the beginning" God created the Heavens and the earth. Indeed we declare, announce and define, that it is altogether necessary to salvation for every human creature to be subject to the Roman pontiff. The Lateran, Nov. 14, in our 8th year. As a perpetual memorial of this matter.

— 71 —

THE LAW *LICET JURIS*, 1338[1]

Emperor Louis IV struggled with Pope John XXII who claimed he had usurped the imperial throne. The emperor maintained that election and not papal approval was all that was necessary. The emperor was finally crowned by an antipapal party which included Marsiglio of Padua who stated in his book Defensor Pacis *that the state was supreme over the church. The German princes supported Louis. Their claim that the person elected King of the Romans was able to rule the empire, and the pope merely had the right of crowning him, is stated below.*

✓   ✓   ✓

Although the proofs of both kinds of law [civil and canon] manifestly declare that the imperial dignity and power proceeded from of old directly through the Son of God, and that God openly gave laws to the human race through the emperor and the kings of the world; and since the emperor is made true emperor by the election alone of those to whom it pertains, and needs not the confirmation or approbation of any one else, since on earth he has no superior as to temporal things, but to him peoples and nations are subject, and our Lord Jesus Christ Himself ordered to be rendered unto God the things that are God's, and unto Caesar the things that are Caesar's; because, nevertheless, some, led by the blindness of avarice and ambition, and having no understanding of Scripture, but turning away from the path of right feeling into certain iniquitous and wicked deceptions, and, breaking forth into detestable assertions, do wage war against the imperial power and authority and against the prerogatives of the emperors, electors, and other princes,

[1] Henderson, *Documents*, pp. 437-439.

and of the faithful subjects of the empire, falsely asserting that the imperial dignity and power come from the
pope and that he who is elected emperor is not true
emperor or king unless he be first confirmed and crowned
through the pope or the apostolic see; and since, through
such wicked assertions and pestiferous dogmas the ancient
enemy moves discord, excites quarrels, prepares dissensions and brings about seditions:—therefore, for the purpose of averting such evil, by the counsel and consent
of the electors and of the other princes of the empire we
declare that the imperial dignity and power comes directly
from God alone; and that, by the old and approved right
and custom of the empire, after any one is chosen as
emperor or king by the electors of the empire concordantly, or by the greater part of them, he is, in consequence
of the election alone, to be considered and called true
king and emperor of the Romans, and he ought to be
obeyed by all the subjects of the empire. And he shall
have full power of administering the laws of the empire
and of doing the other things that pertain to a true emperor; nor does he need the approbation, confirmation,
authority or consent of the apostolic see or of any one
else.

And therefore we decree by this law, to be forever
valid, that he who is elected emperor concordantly or by
the majority of the electors, shall, in consequence of the
election alone, be considered and regarded by all as the
true and lawful emperor; and that he ought to be obeyed
by all the subjects of the empire, and that he shall have,
and shall be considered and firmly asserted by all to have
and to hold, the imperial administration and jurisdiction
and the plenitude of the imperial power. . . .

— 72 —

VENETIAN TRADE WITH THE MONGOLS, AFTER 1345 [1]

Christian merchants in Italy and Southern France maintained commercial relations for the greater part of the medieval period with the infidel. This document is one of a multitude of examples. It also reveals the confusion that arose because of different standards of money, weights, and measures. But this was no real impediment to the trade, for a host of European cities and feudatories had their own separate coinage and weights and measures. Sarai on the lower Volga was the capital of the Golden Horde.

✓   ✓   ✓

In Sarai all linen is sold by *picho*. And 100 *pichi* are equal to 118 *braza* in Venice.

Also, all silks are sold by the *mena*. And the said *mena* is equal to 6 lbs. 2 ozs. minute in Venice. And [silks] are sold at [so many] pounds in cash the *mena,* and all other wares [are sold] the same way. One pound [in cash] they reckon as 6 *tamgha*. And usually £20 circulate and are paid [in exchange] for one *sumo*.

Also, all spices, coral, and other wares are sold by another [kind of] *mena*. And 20 *mene* they reckon as 1 *kanter*. And the said *mena* is equal to 8 lbs. minute in Venice, so that the *kanter* [of this standard] corresponds to 160 lbs. minute in Venice.

Spun gold is sold at the rate of [so many] pounds in cash per bundle, which [bundle] weighs ½ lb. in Venice.

[1] R. S. Lopez and I. W. Raymond, trans., *Medieval Trade in the Mediterranean World* (Records of Civilization, LII, Columbia University Press, New York, 1955), pp. 152-153.

It also is sold at the rate of [so many] *sumi* in cash per ten bundles.

Gauzes and camlets are sold by the piece [of cloth]. And [actual] payments are made in silver *tamgha,* which is their coinage. And for one *sumo* [of account] 120 *tamgha* [in cash] are counted.

Paper is sold by ream and paid in *sumi,* and also at [so many] pounds in cash per ream.

Leather is sold by hundred [piece] lots.

And horsehides are sold at [so many] *tamgha* in cash a piece.

It should be noted that the weights and measures of Astrakhan are like those of Sarai.

— 73 —

THE BLACK DEATH, 1348[1]

The following extracts from the Chronicle of Henry Knighton show some of the consequences of the Black Death. Although he was only a boy when the plague struck England, there is no reason to doubt his memory. On the average, about one-third to one-half of the population of Europe died in two years. It is not difficult to imagine the psychological, social, and economic consequences of such a catastrophe.

✓ ✓ ✓

In this [1348] and the following year there was a general death of people throughout the world. It began first in India, then it passed to Tharsis, thence to the

[1] *Chronicon Henrici Knighton* (J. R. Lumby, ed., Rolls Series, 1895), II, 58-65, *passim.*

Saracens, Christians and Jews in the course of one year, from one Easter to the next. . . .

In one day there died 812 people in Avignon according to the reckoning made to the pope. . . . 358 Dominicans died in Provence in Lent; in Montpellier only seven friars were left from 149. . . . At Marseilles only one Franciscan remained of 150. . . .

Then the grievous plague came to the seacoasts from Southampton, and came to Bristol, and it was there as if all the strength of the town had died, as if they had been hit with sudden death, for there were few who stayed in their beds more than three days, or two days or even one half a day. Then the death broke out everywhere the sun goes. And more than 380 died at Leicester in the small parish of St. Leonard. More than 400 died in the parish of the Holy Cross; 700 died in the parish of St. Margaret of Leicester. And so it was in greater number in each parish. Then the bishop of Lincoln sent throughout his diocese and gave general power to each and every priest, regular as well as secular, to hear confessions and absolve with full and complete episcopal authority, except only in the instance of debt. In which case, if he was able by himself while he lived he should pay it, or others surely would do this for him from his possessions after his death. Likewise the pope granted full remission of all sins to whoever was absolved while in peril of death, and he granted this power to last from Easter to the next following. And everyone could elect his confessor as it pleased him. In this year there was a great pestilence among the sheep everywhere in the kingdom; so that in one place more than 500 sheep died in one pasture, and they became so putrid that neither beasts nor birds would touch them. And because of the fear of death there were low prices for everything. . . . For a man could have one horse which before was worth 40s. for one half a mark. . . . And sheep and cattle wandered through fields and among crops and there was no one who was concerned to drive and collect them, but an unknown number died in ditches and hedges throughout every region for lack of herders. For there was such a lack of servants and helpers that there was no one who knew what he ought to do. . . .

The workers, nevertheless, were so elated and contrary that they did not heed the mandate of the king [prohibiting higher wages] but if anyone wanted to hire them, he had to give them as they desired; either lose their crops and fruit or grant the selfish and lofty wishes of the workers. . . .

After the aforesaid pestilence, many large and small buildings in all the cities, boroughs and villages collapsed and were levelled with the earth for lack of inhabitants; likewise many villages and hamlets were deserted. No house was left in them for everyone who had lived in them had died, and it was probable that many such villages were never to be inhabited again. . . .

— 74 —

THE STATUTE OF LABORERS, 1349[1]

The Black Death struck Europe in 1348 and quickly killed a substantial portion of the population. The ensuing labor shortage resulted in higher wages for workmen and higher prices for goods. But soon employers, including landowners, in order to cut their costs, wished to push wages back to the level before the plague. This is the intent of this statute, and it is in a sense a maximum wage law. But it was hard to enforce, and in 1351 another and similar statute tried to remedy the situation. This legislation, however, did not prevent the Great Revolt of 1381 of peasants and artisans.

✓   ✓   ✓

Edward [III] by the grace of God etc. . . have ordained:

[1] *Statutes of the Realm* (1810), I, 307-308, with minor emendations.

That every man and woman of our realm of England, of what condition he be, free or bond, able in body and within the age of threescore years, not living in merchandise, nor exercising any craft, nor having of his own whereof he may live, nor proper land, about whose tillage he may occupy himself, and not serving any other, if he is in suitable service, his station considered, be required to serve, he shall be bounden to serve him who so shall him require; and take only the wages, livery, meed or salary which were accustomed to be given in the places where he oweth to serve, the twentieth year of our reign of England, or five or six other common years next before. Provided always, that the lords be preferred before others in their bondmen or their land tenants to be retained in their service: so that, nevertheless, the said lords shall retain no more than necessary for them; and if any such man or woman, being so required to serve, will not do this, and this being proved by two true men before the sheriff (or the bailiffs of our sovereign lord, the king, or the constables) of the town where this shall happen to be done, he shall anon be taken by them, or any of them, and committed to the next jail, there to remain under straight keeping till he find surety to serve in the form aforesaid.

Item, If any reaper, mower, or other workman or servant, of whatever estate or condition that he be, retained in any man's service, do depart from the said service without reasonable cause or license before the term agreed, he shall have the penalty of imprisonment. And that none, under the same penalty, presume to receive or retain any such person in his service.

Item, That no man pay or promise to pay any servant any more wages, liveries, meed or salary than was wont as afore is said; nor that any in any other manner shall demand or receive the same, upon pain of doubling the sum that so shall be paid, promised, required, or received to him which thereof shall feel himself grieved; and if none such will prosecute then the sum is to be applied to any of the people that will prosecute; and such prosecution shall be in the court of the lord of the place where such case shall happen.

Item, If the lords of the towns or manors presume in

any point to come against this present ordinance, either themselves or their servants, then suit shall be made against them in the counties, wapentakes, tithings or such other courts for treble penalty of the sum paid or promised by them or their servants, in the form aforesaid; and if any, before this present ordinance hath covenanted with anyone so to serve for more wages, he shall not be bound by reason of the same covenant, to pay more than at another time was wont to be paid to such person; nor upon the said penalty shall he presume to pay any more.

Item, That saddlers, skinners, white-tawers, cordwainers, tailors, smiths, carpenters, masons, tilers, shipwrights, carters and all other artificers and workmen shall not take for their labor and workmanship above the same that was wont to be paid to such persons in the said twentieth year, and other common years next before, as afore is said, in the place where they shall happen to work; and if any man take more, he shall be committed to the nearest jail in the manner as afore is said.

Item, That butchers, fishmongers, hostlers, brewers, bakers, pulters and all other sellors of all manner of victual shall be bound to sell the same victual for a reasonable price, having respect to the price that such victual be sold at in the adjoining places, so that the same sellors have moderate gains, and not excessive, reasonably to be required according to the distance of the place from whence the said victual be carried. . . .

Item, Because many strong beggars as long as they may live of begging do refuse to labor, giving themselves to idleness and vice, and sometime to theft and other abominations; none, under the said pain of imprisonment shall under the color of pity or alms give anything to such who may possibly labor, or presume to favor them in their sloth, so that thereby they may be compelled to labor for their necessary living.

— 75 —

THE GOLDEN BULL, 1356[1]

In the century following the death of Frederick II in 1250, the princes, lay and ecclesiastical, of Germany had gathered to themselves practically all the powers of the German crown that he had not already granted away. The imperial and royal title remained as an anachronism. Of all the princes and nobles, the seven who elected the Holy Roman Emperor were in many ways pre-eminent. Emperor Charles IV undertook to define this group, ascribe certain functions to it, and obtain privileges for his kingdom of Bohemia in the Golden Bull, which is a kind of fundamental law.

✓   ✓   ✓

CHAPTER I

Escort and Safe-Conduct for the Electors

1. We decree and determine by this imperial edict that, whenever the electoral princes are summoned according to the ancient and praiseworthy custom to meet and elect a king of the Romans and future emperor, each one of them shall be bound to furnish on demand an escort and safe-conduct to his fellow electors or their representatives, within his own lands and as much farther as he can, for the journey to and from the city where the election is to be held. Any electoral prince who refuses to furnish escort and safe-conduct shall be liable to the penalties for perjury and to the loss of his electoral vote for that occasion.

2. We decree and command also that all other princes who hold fiefs from the empire by whatever title, and all

---

[1] Thatcher and McNeal, *Source Book*, pp. 284-305, *passim.* Reprinted by permission of the publisher.

counts, barons, knights, clients, nobles, commoners, citizens, and all corporations of towns, cities, and territories of the empire, shall furnish escort and safe-conduct for this occasion to every electoral prince or his representatives, on demand, within their own lands and as much farther as they can. . . .

6. If any electoral prince violates any of the above or following laws of the empire, he shall be excluded by his fellow-electors from their body, and shall be deprived of his vote and his electoral dignity, and of his right to hold fiefs of the empire. If any other prince of any rank or station, or any count, baron, or noble who holds fiefs of the empire, or any of their successors to their fiefs, is guilty of a similar crime, he shall not be invested with the fiefs which he holds of the empire, nor be able to receive a fief from any other lord, and he shall incur the above penalties, according to his rank.

7. The above rules apply to escorts and safe-conduct in general, but we have thought it well to indicate also the neighboring lands which should furnish escort and safe-conduct: [These follow].

15. It shall be the duty of the archbishop of Mainz to send notice of the approaching election to each of the electoral princes by his messenger bearing letters patent. . . .

16. When the news of the death of the king of the Romans has been received at Mainz, within one month from the date of receiving it the archbishop of Mainz shall send notices of the death and of the approaching election to all the electoral princes. But if the archbishop neglects or refuses to send such notices, the electoral princes are commanded on their fidelity to assemble on their own motion and without summons at the city of Frankfort within three months from the death of the emperor, for the purpose of electing a king of the Romans and future emperor.

CHAPTER II

The Election of the King of the Romans

2. [The other electors repeat this oath after the archbishop of Mainz.] "I, archbishop of Mainz, archchancellor

of the empire for Germany, electoral prince, swear on the holy gospels here before me, and by the faith which I owe to God and to the holy Roman empire, that with the aid of God, and according to my best judgment and knowledge, I will cast my vote, in this election of the king of the Romans and future emperor, for a person fitted to rule the Christian people. I will give my voice and vote freely, uninfluenced by any agreement, price, bribe, promise, or anything of the sort, by whatever name it may be called. So help me God and all the saints."

3. After the electors have taken this oath, they shall proceed to the election, and shall not depart from Frankfort until the majority have elected a king of the Romans and future emperor, to be ruler of the world and of the Christian people. . . .

CHAPTER VII

The Succession of the Electoral Princes

1. . . . It is known and recognized throughout the world, that the king of Bohemia, the count Palatine of the Rhine, the duke of Saxony, and the margrave of Brandenburg, by virtue of the principalities which they possess, have the right to vote in the election of the king of the Romans along with their coelectors, the ecclesiastical princes, and that they with the ecclesiastical princes are the true and legal electoral princes of the holy empire. In order to prevent disputes arising among the sons of these secular electoral princes in regard to the electoral authority and vote, which would be productive of delays dangerous to the state and other evils, we have fixed the succession by the present law which shall be valid forever. . . .

2. When any electorate falls vacant for lack of heirs, the emperor or king of the Romans shall have the power to dispose of it, as if it reverted to the empire, saving the rights, privileges, and customs of the kingdom of Bohemia, according to which the inhabitants of that kingdom have the right to elect their king in case of a vacancy.

CHAPTER XII

Assemblies of the Princes

. . . It has been decided in the general diet held at
Nürnberg with the electoral princes, ecclesiastical and
secular, and other princes and magnates, by their advice
and with their consent, that in the future, the electoral
princes shall meet every year in some city of the empire
four weeks after Easter; this year they are to meet at that
date in the imperial city of Metz. . . .

CHAPTER XXI

The Precedence Among the Archbishops

We have defined above the location of the seats of the
ecclesiastical electors in the council, at the table, and on
other occasions, when the emperor meets with the electoral princes, but we have thought it well to indicate also
the order of precedence in procession and march. Therefore we decree by the present imperial edict that whenever the emperor or king of the Romans meets with the
electoral princes, and the insignia are borne before him in
procession, the archbishop of Trier shall march directly
before the emperor or king, no one being between them
except the bearers of the insignia; and when the emperor
or king marches without the insignia the archbishop shall
immediately precede him. The other two archbishops (of
Mainz and Cologne) shall march on either side of the
archbishop of Trier, their position on the right or the left
being determined by the region in which the ceremony is
held. . . .

CHAPTER XXII

The Order of Precedence Among the Secular Electoral Princes, and the Bearers of the Insignia

We also determine by the present decree the precedence among the secular electoral princes as follows:
When the electoral princes march in procession with the
emperor or king of the Romans in any of the ceremonies
of the imperial diet and the insignia are borne before him,

the duke of Saxony shall precede the emperor or king, marching between him and the archbishop of Trier, and bearing the imperial or royal sword; the count palatine of the Rhine shall march at the right of the duke of Saxony with the imperial globe, and the margrave of Brandenburg at the left with the sceptre; the king of Bohemia shall follow immediately behind the emperor or king.

PART II

(Published at Metz, December 25, 1356)

CHAPTER XXV

If it is proper that the integrity of the ordinary principalities should be preserved, for the better securing of justice and peace for the subjects, it is even more important that the great principalities of the electoral princes should be kept intact in their domains, honors, and rights. Therefore we determine and decree by this imperial edict that the lands, districts, fiefs, and other possessions of the great principalities, namely, the kingdom of Bohemia, the palatinate of the Rhine, the duchy of Saxony, and the mark of Brandenburg, should never under any circumstances be separated, divided, or dismembered. In order that they may be preserved in their integrity, the firstborn son in each case shall succeed to them, and shall exercise ownership and dominion in them, unless he be incapacitated for ruling by reason of imbecility, or other notorious defect. In that case, he shall not be allowed to inherit, but the succession shall go to the nearest male lay heir on the paternal side. . . .

CHAPTER XXIX

1. We have learned from records and traditions, that it has been the custom in the past to hold the election of the king of the Romans in Frankfort, the coronation in Aachen, and the first diet in Nürnberg; therefore we decree that in the future these ceremonies shall be held in these places, unless there shall be some legitimate obstacle. . . .

— 76 —

JOHN WYCLIFFE ON CONFESSION[1]

Perhaps the best-known work of John Wycliffe (ca. 1324-1384) is his translation of the bible into English, yet this was not as serious to his contemporaries as his ideas on the doctrine of the Church. One of the errors which were regarded as heretical was his view of confession. The example below illustrates this, but also shows how, like later reformers, he went back to the early practices of the church for precedents, or lack thereof.

✠ ✠ ✠

To make holiness in men is confession needful. . . . Confession generally is acknowledging made with will; and some confession is made without sin, and some is acknowledging of sin; and both these are good for man, but the first is more worthy in Christ. Matthew telleth how Christ confessed to his Father, lord of this world, and that Christ might not sin, and this confession might not be vain. Confession that man maketh of sin is made of man in two manners. Some is made only to God truly by heart or mouth. And some confession is made to man, and that may be in many manners; either openly and generally, as men confessed in the old law; or privily and whisperingly as men confess nowadays. When a man is constrained by bodily pain to tell his guilt, he confesseth not; but confession must be wilful, or else it is not helpful to man.

It were to know besides in this matter, whether privy confession made to priests be needful to sinful men and whether this confession is grounded. And it seemeth that

[1] John Wycliffe, *De Confessione,* in F. D. Matthew, Ed., *The Works of Wyclif, Hitherto Unprinted* (Early English Text Society, London, 1880), Vol. 74, pp. 327-329. The spelling has been modernized.

it is not needful, but brought in late by the devil; for omniscient Christ used it not, nor any of his apostles after. And if it were needful to man, Christ would have used it or taught it. . . . And thus it seemeth to many men that Christian men might well be saved without such confession; as they were before pope Innocent, and thus it seemeth presumption of this pope to make this law; for holy church should not thus be charged with new laws, when old suffice. . . .

— 77 —

CHURCH ABUSES DRAWN UP BY THE COUNCIL OF CONSTANCE, 1417[1]

The Council of Constance healed the Schism and condemned John Huss, but the true state of ecclesiastical affairs is perhaps better illustrated by the following list of abuses. These eighteen points were presented to the new Pope Martin V for his action, but as it turned out he had no interest in them.

The Council orders, that the future Pope shall, in concert with the said council, or with the deputies of the nations . . . reform the church in its head . . . : 1. Concerning the number, quality, and the nation of the cardinals. 2. Concerning the reservations of the Holy See. 3. Concerning the annates, the common and small fees. 4. Concerning the collations to benefices, and the expecta-

[1] James Lenfant, *The History of the Council of Constance* (London, 1730), II, 145-146.

tive favors or reversions. 5. Concerning the confirmation of elections. 6. Concerning what causes ought, or ought not, to be pleaded at the court of Rome. 7. Concerning appellations, or appeals to the said court. 8. Concerning the offices of the Chancery and Penitentiary. 9. Concerning the exemptions and unions, or incorporations, made during the Schism. 10. Concerning *Commendams*. 11. Concerning . . . revenues during the vacancy of b nefices. 12. Against the alienation of the estates of the church of Rome, and other churches. 13. Concerning the causes for which a Pope may be corrected and deposed, and how. 14. Concerning the extirpation of simony. 15. Concerning dispensations. 16. Concerning the provisions for the Pope and cardinals. 17. Concerning indulgences. 18. Concerning the tenths.

— 78 —

THE SENTENCE AGAINST JOAN OF ARC, 1431[1]

The story of the maiden Joan is too well known to be repeated here. In a society where errors against the church go unpunished, it is difficult to recapture the feeling against Joan. Besides, in the eyes of the English, and their allies, she was a dangerous enemy who must not be allowed to leave their prison. From the church's point of view, Joan compounded her misfortunes when having agreed to submit, she then relapsed into heresy. This placed her beyond the pale. New insight into the story of Joan may be read in Jean Bosler, "Was Joan of Arc

---

[1] Pierre Champion, *Procès de condamnation de Jeanne d'Arc* (2 vols., Paris, 1921), II, 299-300.

Charles VII's Sister?" Cambridge Journal, *Vol. VII, No. 12 (September, 1954), pp. 756-776.*

✓   ✓   ✓

In the name of the Father, amen. Every time that the pestilential poison of heresy firmly afflicts one of the members of the Church and changes him into an agent of Satan, one must watch very diligently that the wicked contagion of this pernicious filth is not introduced into the other members of the mystical body of Christ. The decrees of the holy fathers have prescribed also that hardened heretics must be separated from the company of the just, as much to let these pernicious vipers be rekindled in the breast of our pious mother church as for the grave danger incurred by the other faithful.

Therefore, we, Pierre, by divine mercy bishop of Beauvais, and brother Jean Le Maistre, vicar of the worthy doctor Jean Graverent, inquisitor of heretical error, and specially deputized by him in this case, lawful judges in this region, have declared by impartial judgment that you, Joan, commonly called the Maiden. have fallen into various errors and diverse crimes of schism, idolatry, invocation of demons, and several other misdeeds. However, since the church does not close its lap to those who return to her, feeling that with pure thought and a strong faith that you would be separated from your errors and crimes, since, on a certain day, you renounced them, publicly made an oath and vows and promises never to return to these errors or any heresy, in any manner whatsoever or under any influence at all, but rather to live firmly in the unity of the Catholic church and the communion of the Roman pontiff, even as is more fully explained in the document signed by your own hand; considering that in the course of time, after the abjuration of your errors, the cause of the schism and heresy broke forth in your heart which it had seduced, and that you had relapsed, O sorrow! into those errors and crimes, just as a dog returns to its vomit, even as appears abundantly and evidently from your spontaneous confessions and statements, we have recognized by very well known sentences that, with feint heart rather than with a true and faithful spirit you have denied only with your mouth your previous inventions and errors.

For these reasons we declare to you that you have relapsed into your former errors and, under the blow of the sentence of excommunication that you had incurred previously, we judge that you are a relapsed heretic. And by this sentence which, sitting on this court, we bear by this document and state, we deem that, for such a rotted limb, in order that it not infect the other limbs of Christ, you are to be cut off from the unity of the said church, severed from its body and that you must be handed over to the secular power. And we reject you, cut you away, abandon you, praying that this same secular power may temper its sentence on you, short of death and mutilation of limbs; and if real signs of repentance appear in you, that the sacrament of penance be administered to you.

— 79 —

THE END OF THE HUNDRED YEARS' WAR, 1451 [1]

The French were able to drive the English from all of France except Calais in the twenty years following the death of Joan of Arc. No treaty of peace between Charles VII (1422-1461) and Henry VI (1422-1461) was signed; both sides just stopped fighting. Perhaps the following brief notice by a chronicler of this fact is symbolic of the exhaustion of both antagonists. The last battle of the war was actually fought in 1453, when Bordeaux fell.

✠   ✠   ✠

Thus by the grace and aid of God the duchy of Aquitaine, very soon thereafter that of Normandy and in gen-

[1] Jehan de Waurin, *Recueil des Chroniques* (Rolls Series, London, 1891), V, 193.

eral all the kingdom of France, except the city of Calais which is still in the hands of the English, were reduced to obedience of the King of France. May God grant that everything will soon be returned so that the words of the scripture will be done which says: obedience is better than sacrifice.

— 80 —

THE MERCHANT, 1458[1]

The selection below was written by a merchant in Naples. It is almost exactly contemporary with the fall of Constantinople and the end of the Hundred Years' War. The status of the merchants had changed appreciably in 400 years, perhaps more than it would in the following centuries. Their rise to a position where they would dominate the feudal lords of Europe is an important aspect of medieval history.

The dignity and office of merchants is great and exalted in many respects, and most particularly in four. First, with respect to the common weal. For the advancement of public welfare is a very honorable [purpose], as Cicero states, and one ought [to be willing] even to die [for it]. . . . The advancement, the comfort, and the health of republics to a large extent proceed from merchants; we are always speaking, of course, not of plebeian and vulgar merchants but of the glorious merchant of

[1] R. S. Lopez and I. W. Raymond, trans., *Medieval Trade in the Mediterranean World* (Records of Civilization, LII, Columbia University Press, New York, 1955), pp. 416-418.

whom we treat [and who is] lauded in this work of ours. And with respect to mercantile business and activity [we may say] this: Through trade, that ornament and advancement [of republics], sterile countries are provided with food and supplies and also enjoy many strange things which are imported from places where [other] commodities are lacking. [Merchants] also bring about an abundance of money, jewels, gold, silver, and all kinds of metals. They bring about an abundance of gilds of various crafts. Hence, cities and countries are driven to cultivate the land, to enlarge the herds, and to exploit the incomes and rents. And [merchants] through their activity enable the poor to live; through their initiative in tax farming they promote the activity of administrators; through their exports and imports of merchandise they cause the customs and excises of the lords and republics to expand, and consequently they enlarge the public and common treasury.

Secondly, I exalt the dignity and office of merchants with respect to the useful and honorable management of their private properties and goods. As a matter of fact, a sparing, temperate, solid, and upright merchant increases and augments his wealth. This is why we observe that merchants abound in movable and immovable property, in the wealth of their homes and furniture, in the ornaments and clothing of their families, in the dowering of their sons and daughters, and consequently in the continuous improvement of their condition through intermarriage with ever higher [families]. . . .

Third, the dignity of merchants is to be esteemed and appreciated with respect to association, both private and public. Private [association] means at home, where [the merchant] associates with an honorable family in continuous and virtuous activity. For you have to consider that where silver, gold, money, and other things of similar value are handled, there is no room for rogues, retainers, henchmen of all sorts, partisans, thieves, runaways, and gamblers such as are wont to live at the courts of princes, magnates, and lords. . . . Outside their homes, merchants associate with artisans, gentlemen, lords, princes, and prelates of every rank, all of whom flock [to see] the merchants since they always need them. And very frequently great scholars come to visit merchants in their homes. . . . For no professional [man] understands or has ever understood the monarchies of this world and the states in regard to management of money—upon which all human states depend—as does a good and learned merchant. . . .

We have left for the fourth [place] the dignity of merchants with respect to [good] faith. . . . It is generally said that today [good] faith abides with merchants and men-at-arms. . . . Neither kings nor princes nor any [other] rank of men enjoy as much reputation or credit as a good merchant. Hence, a merchant's [reputation and credit] serve him readily for cash, while those of others do not: and if they [i.e. the credit and reputation of others] are given in payment, they carry a much higher interest [charge than the merchants']. And whereas a simple and plain receipt of a merchant is valid even without witnesses, the rulers and any other people are not believed without an instrument and strong caution. Hence, and for the reasons [already] given, merchants ought to take pride in their outstanding dignity.

And to proceed according to our design we shall state that in order to maintain this dignity it is necessary for a merchant to remove from himself any undignified ornament both of the soul and of the body. And merchants must not have the fierce manners of husky men-at-arms, nor must they have the soft manners of jesters and comedians, but they must be serious in speaking, in walking, and in all actions, maintaining as much as possible their dignity. . . .

INDEX

(N.B. In general nouns and subjects mentioned in the Table of Contents do not appear below.)

VAN NOSTRAND ANVIL BOOKS already published